THINGS TO DO IN FORT LAUDERDALE BEFORE YOU DIE

Hillsboro Lighthouse
Photo courtesy of Anthony J Rayburn, anthonyjrayburn.com

100 THINGS TO DO IN FORT LAUDERDALE BEFORE YOU DIE

CHRISTIANA LILLY

Reedy Press
PO Box 5131
St. Louis, MO 63139, USA
www.reedypress.com

Library of Congress Control Number: 2022936992

ISBN: 9781681063843

Design by Jill Halpin

All images were provided by the author unless otherwise noted.

Printed in the United States of America
22 23 24 25 26   5 4 3 2 1

We (the publisher and the author) have done our best to provide the most accurate information available when this book was completed. However, we make no warranty, guarantee, or promise about the accuracy, completeness, or currency of the information provided, and we expressly disclaim all warranties, express or implied. Please note that attractions, company names, addresses, websites, and phone numbers are subject to change or closure, and this is outside of our control. We are not responsible for any loss, damage, injury, or inconvenience that may occur due to the use of this book. When exploring new destinations, please do your homework before you go. You are responsible for your own safety and health when using this book.

DEDICATION

For Jack, my Fort Lauderdale boy

A Wreck Bar mermaid at the B Ocean Resort

CONTENTS

Music and Entertainment

Sports and Recreation

Culture and History

Shopping and Fashion

PREFACE

The Venice of America, Spring Break central, the Yachting Capital of the World—Fort Lauderdale is a city of many faces.

It earned these monikers over the years as it explored its identity, growing from a boggy riverfront community to a place where co-eds flock to the beach, where celebrities escape from the hubbub of life to enjoy a tropical drink at the Wreck Bar or Mai Kai, and northerners who've had enough of the winter weather traded snowflakes for seashells. But even before then, trailblazers like Frank and Ivy Stranahan set out for the New River, their humble green-and-white abode still standing strong as it becomes sandwiched between high-rises. And hundreds of years before the arrival of pioneers, the Seminole people made their indelible mark on Fort Lauderdale and South Florida.

I moved from Miami Beach to Fort Lauderdale in 2009, back when rent for a one-bedroom apartment was more easily affordable. While I was born in Florida, I was not raised here and that's allowed me to view the state and my adopted home with childlike wonder. In coming up with 100 things to do in Fort Lauderdale (before you die, of course) I got to experience the all the facets of what make the city so special. I polled locals and transplants about their top spots to take friends and family when they're in town and jotted down places, experiences, and tastes that I had personally accumulated over the years. And by simply driving down Broward Boulevard, US-1, and A1A, I found places that needed to be included in this book while adding them to my own list of things to do.

Whether you decided to make Fort Lauderdale your home later in life, were born at Broward General and know the streets of Fort Lauderdale like the back of your hand, or are on vacation for a long weekend, I hope you enjoy this book and are invigorated by everything it has to offer.

And for everyone reading it, know that this book could have easily been "1,000 Things to Do in Fort Lauderdale before You Die."

ACKNOWLEDGMENTS

It takes more than one person to put together a guidebook on a city as rich as Fort Lauderdale.

Thank you to the friends and family who recommended places to include, from watering holes and water activities to historic landmarks and exciting annual events.

Thank you also to the cultural institutions who took the time to provide me with private tours or insiders' views of their history, including but not limited to Ah-Tah-Thi-Ki, the Fort Lauderdale Historical Society, Bonnet House Museum & Gardens, and Wreck Bar.

Thank you to everyone who ever invited me out on an adventure to a lauded restaurant, hiking trail, indie marketplace, museum, seminar, or hidden Fort Lauderdale treasure. Little did I know that you were helping me gather ideas and exploits for a book many years later.

Quinoa beet salad at Shooters Waterfront

FOOD AND DRINK

1

EXPLORE
THE YELLOW GREEN FARMERS MARKET

Spices, plants, beauty products, clothing, artwork, dog treats, imported goods and food from around the world . . . what doesn't Yellow Green Farmers Market have? The sprawling market is open every weekend and boasts more than 350 vendors who have all the bases covered, and the proprietor goes out of his way to make sure he doesn't duplicate shops. Once you've found a stand that tickles your taste buds—whether it be vegan treats, pasta made from scratch, BBQ straight from the pit, or Mexican street corn dripping with *cotija* cheese—grab a seat beneath a chickee hut and enjoy the live tunes. Warning: the nearby pit smokers will probably have you going back for seconds in no time. On those especially hot days, opt to pair your meal with a frozen drink or beer from one of the market's bars.

3080 Sheridan St., Hollywood, 954-513-3990
ygfarmersmarket.com

TIP

Wander the aisles before committing to a meal; it's going to be a tough choice. You won't be able to make it to every vendor on your first visit, and that's OK. It just means you'll have to come back soon!

2

ORDER EVERYTHING BUT THE KITCHEN SINK
AT JAXSON'S ICE CREAM PARLOR

With its red-and-white awning, you can't miss Jaxson's. The family-owned joint covered with license plates and road signs only does things big, including the most iconic item on the menu: The Original Kitchen Sink. Served in an actual kitchen sink, the vessel is filled with one pound of ice cream per person and topped with bananas, cherries, mixed nuts, and fluffy homemade whipped cream. Just to add to the drama, two sparklers are lit as the dessert parades through the dining room before arriving at your table. If that's not quite what you're in the mood for, choose from a variety of sundaes, banana splits, shakes, and ice cream soda floats, as well as savory nachos, fries, burgers, hot dogs, and more. Don't forget to stop into their country store for a souvenir before you leave.

128 S Federal Hwy., Dania Beach, 954-923-4445
jaxsonicecream.com

3

PLAY GIANT JENGA
AT FUNKY BUDDHA BREWERY

If there were ever a rags-to-riches story, it's that of the Funky Buddha. The brewery got its start as a strip-mall lounge in Boca Raton in 2007, started brewing beers in 2010, then opened a 54,000-square-foot brewery and tap room in 2013 in Oakland Park. Now, after joining the company that also sells Corona, its beers can be found on shelves across the country, from the classics Last Snow and Floridian to the infamous Maple Bacon Coffee Porter and new-to-the-scene hard seltzers. Beer nuts can also order food from the full menu or join friends in the game room for giant Jenga and cornhole. Don't forget to take a selfie in front of the mural of the brewing process.

1201 NE 38th St., Oakland Park, 954-440-0046
funkybuddhabrewery.com

Fort Lauderdale might be new to the brewery scene compared to other cities around the country, but locals have truly embraced the beers these brewers are creating. Here are five other breweries worth the visit.

Gulf Stream Brewery
1105 NE 13th St., 954-766-4842
gulfstreambeer.com

Holy Mackerel
1414 NE 26th St., 954-300-2631
holymackerelbeers.com

Invasive Species Brewing
726 NE 2nd Ave.
invasivespeciesbrewing.com

LauderAle Brewery
3305 SE 14th Ave., 954-653-9711
lauderale.co

Tarpon River Brewing
280 SW 6th St., 954-353-3193
tarponriverbrewing.com

FEED THE TARPON
AT 15TH STREET FISHERIES

This oceanfront restaurant is a two-for-one deal, with a casual dockside diner on the first floor featuring live music on Fridays, Saturdays, and Sundays, and a more formal upstairs dining room designed to look like a boathouse. Whichever experience/menu you choose, you're in for a treat with dishes like conch chowder, fried gator, grilled swordfish, and pan-seared cobia. Its wine list is impressive, too, winning 15th Street Fisheries an Award of Excellence from *Wine Spectator*. While you're waiting for your food to arrive, walk to the dock to feed the frenzied tarpon fish, an activity the whole family will enjoy. And the dock isn't just there for show—diners can arrive by boat for their lunch or dinner date. The restaurant also has a 24-hour dock cam on its website, so you can watch the boats sail by, no matter where in the world you are.

1900 SE 15th St., 954-763-2777
15streetfisheries.com

RELIVE SPRING BREAK
AT ELBO ROOM

Fort Lauderdale Beach has been a prime Spring Break destination since the rebellious '50s and groovy '60s, and the iconic Elbo Room has served as a welcome mat for the hordes of college students from across the country descending upon its sandy shores. The dive bar was even included in the 1960 rom-com, *Where the Boys Are*, starring Connie Francis and George Hamilton. Elbo Room's doors first opened in 1938, and 80 years later it still attracts throngs of visitors and locals alike looking for a good time. With beers and cocktails served just across the street from the Atlantic Ocean and live music echoing off the walls, you're sure to enjoy your time—day or night—at this Fort Lauderdale icon.

241 S Fort Lauderdale Beach Blvd., 954-463-4615
elboroom.com

6

WATCH THE YACHTS GO BY
AT SHOOTERS

You'd never guess that this swanky restaurant on the Intracoastal was once a dive bar in the 1980s known for wet T-shirt contests and hot tubs. But the restaurant is all grown up now, reinventing itself as a popular evening destination swathed in nautical décor and offering alfresco dining in cabanas and beneath beach umbrellas. While it might not look anything like it did decades ago, it's stayed true to its roots by keeping not only the name Shooters, but also a few black-and-white photos paying homage to yesteryear. Valet your car out front or arrive in style by boat and reserve a slip at the restaurant's docks. As you enjoy a glass of wine and a decadent seafood dish, watch the vessels go by on the Intracoastal—boaters are always greeting diners with a smile and a wave.

3033 NE 32nd Ave., 954-566-2855
shooterswaterfront.com

7

WAIT IN LINE FOR A PUB SUB
AT PUBLIX

Yes, a grocery store has made the cut to be among the 100 things you should do in Fort Lauderdale. The family-owned Publix has been a shopping mainstay for generations of Floridians since its founding in 1930. Since that time, it has become practically mandatory to stop by the deli to get a Pub Sub before heading out to the beach or packing your lunch for a day on the boat. So, head to the nearest Publix (there's one on almost every corner and you can't miss its green logo) and find out which is your favorite sub: is it the chicken tender sub; the Ultimate Sub with ham, turkey breast, and roast beef; or the Smoky Cuban sub? You really can't go wrong, but prepare to defend your favorite to other Pub Sub aficionados.

publix.com

TIP

If you've got little ones with you on your trip to Publix, stop by the bakery section to get each of them a free cookie.

8

ORDER THE COWBOY STEAK

AT TROPICAL ACRES

Tropical Acres has been a Fort Lauderdale institution since 1949 when the restaurant had a four-digit phone number. At the time, the location was considered "out West," but with the menu's juicy steaks and quality service, diners were not deterred by the distance and that led to the opening of three more locations. While the original Tropical Acres is the last one standing, it's considered an icon in Fort Lauderdale dining with its menu of filet mignon, New York strip, bone-in cowboy steak, seafood, pork chops, and pastas. Home chefs who have a knack for cooking steaks can take advantage of the restaurant's butcher shop, which opened in 2020, allowing customers to order cuts of meat ahead of time for pickup and at-home grilling.

2500 Griffin Rd., 954-989-2500
tropicalacres.com

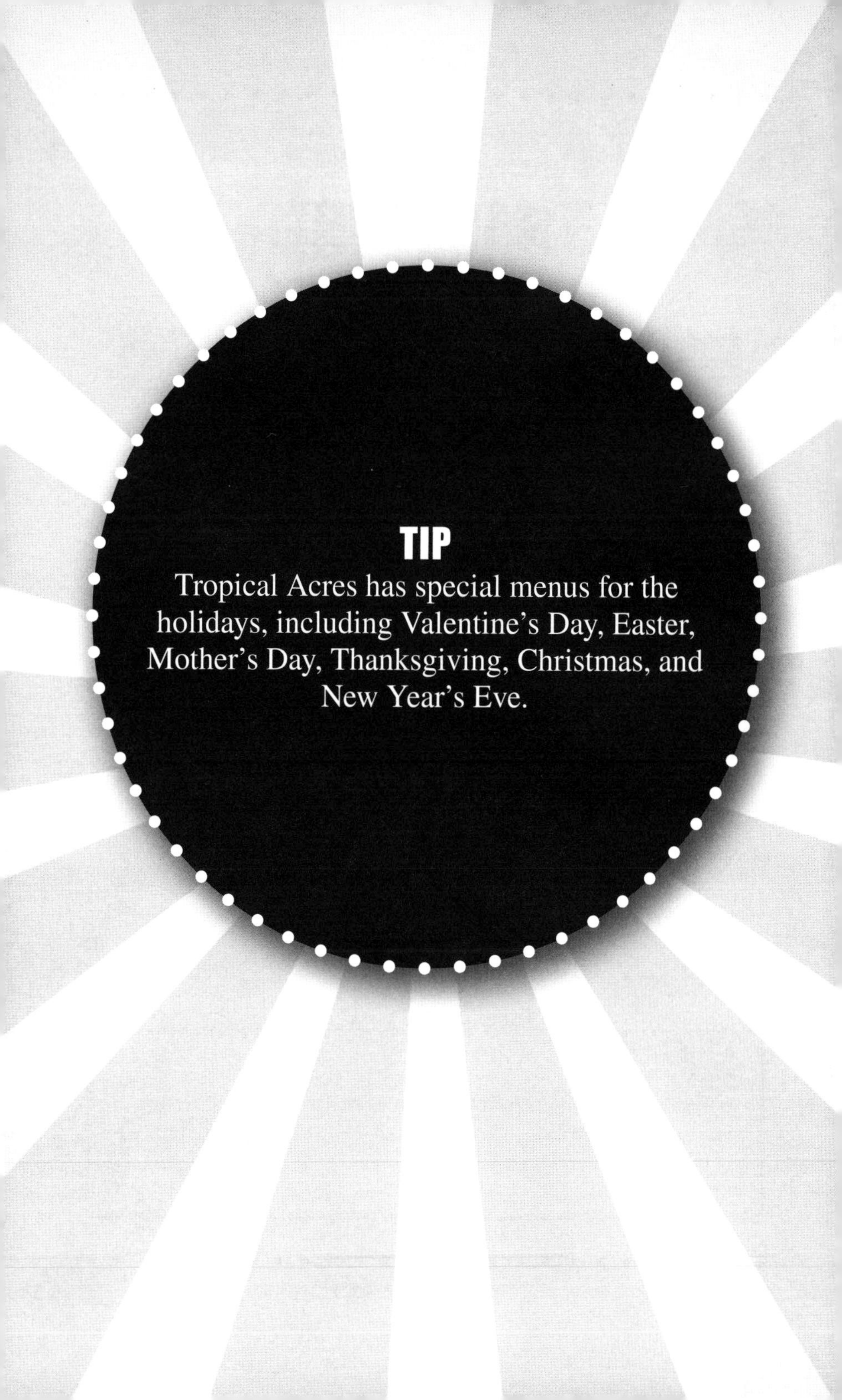
TIP
Tropical Acres has special menus for the holidays, including Valentine's Day, Easter, Mother's Day, Thanksgiving, Christmas, and New Year's Eve.

9

SAVE BIG
DURING DINE OUT LAUDERDALE RESTAURANT MONTHS

August and September are slow months for Greater Fort Lauderdale, as most tourists are back home after enjoying the spring and summer months lounging on the beach. However, if you're sticking around, you'll be rewarded with dining deals during the annual Dine Out Lauderdale Restaurant Months. Participating restaurants throughout Broward County create set menus for just $35 and $45, allowing diners to indulge in delicious eats at some of our favorite locales. Think high-end steakhouses and seafood eateries usually saved for special occasions. Set your game plan for dinner by cruising the Visit Lauderdale website, sunny.org, to see which restaurants are participating.

sunny.org

TIP

Miami-Dade and Palm Beach Counties, as well as individual municipalities, also have their own dining specials during this time period, so you can eat your way through South Florida without breaking the bank.

HAVE BREAKFAST ALL DAY LONG
AT THE FLORIDIAN

You don't have to be a Floridian to enjoy what they're serving at this 24-hour breakfast spot on Las Olas Boulevard. Since 1937—that's ancient by South Florida standards—"The Flo" has been serving hearty helpings of breakfast favorites like pancakes, French toast, omelets, breakfast wraps, and eggs Benedict, as well as meatloaf, New York strip steak, pork chops, and dozens of types of sandwiches. And because breakfast is not complete without a little bubbly, bottles of Dom Perignon are also on the menu, as part of the "Fat Cat" Breakfast for two consisting of New York strip steak, two eggs, home fries or grits, toast or a biscuit, and a bottle of the good stuff—or pay less for the cheap stuff if you go for the "Not So Fat Cat" Breakfast meal. Either way, you'll feel as ritzy as the celebrities whose photos cover the walls of this classic Florida institution.

1410 E Las Olas Blvd., 954-463-4041
thefloridiandiner.com

11

FIND YOUR FAVORITE DOUGHNUT FLAVOR

AT DANDEE DONUT FACTORY

Move over, big chain doughnuts. Dandee Donut Factory is a breakfast institution in Greater Fort Lauderdale, with oversized pastries in more than 50 decadent flavors. Compare old faithfuls like powdered sugar, jelly filled, apple crumb, and chocolate frosted doughnuts to the likes of the s'mores, Snickers, white coconut, and maple bacon flavors. Order your breakfast to go or enjoy a seat in the diner or outside under an umbrella. And if you're not a morning person, don't worry: you can get your fix of doughnuts, coffee, and other breakfast items from the diner menu whenever you want—Dandee Donuts' stores are open 24 hours a day, seven days a week at its three locations in Margate, Deerfield Beach, and the original Pompano Beach storefront.

1900 Atlantic Blvd., Pompano Beach, 954-785-1461
1422 S Federal Hwy., Deerfield Beach, 954-531-1990
3101 N State Rd. 7, Margate, 754-444-3157

dandeedonuts.com

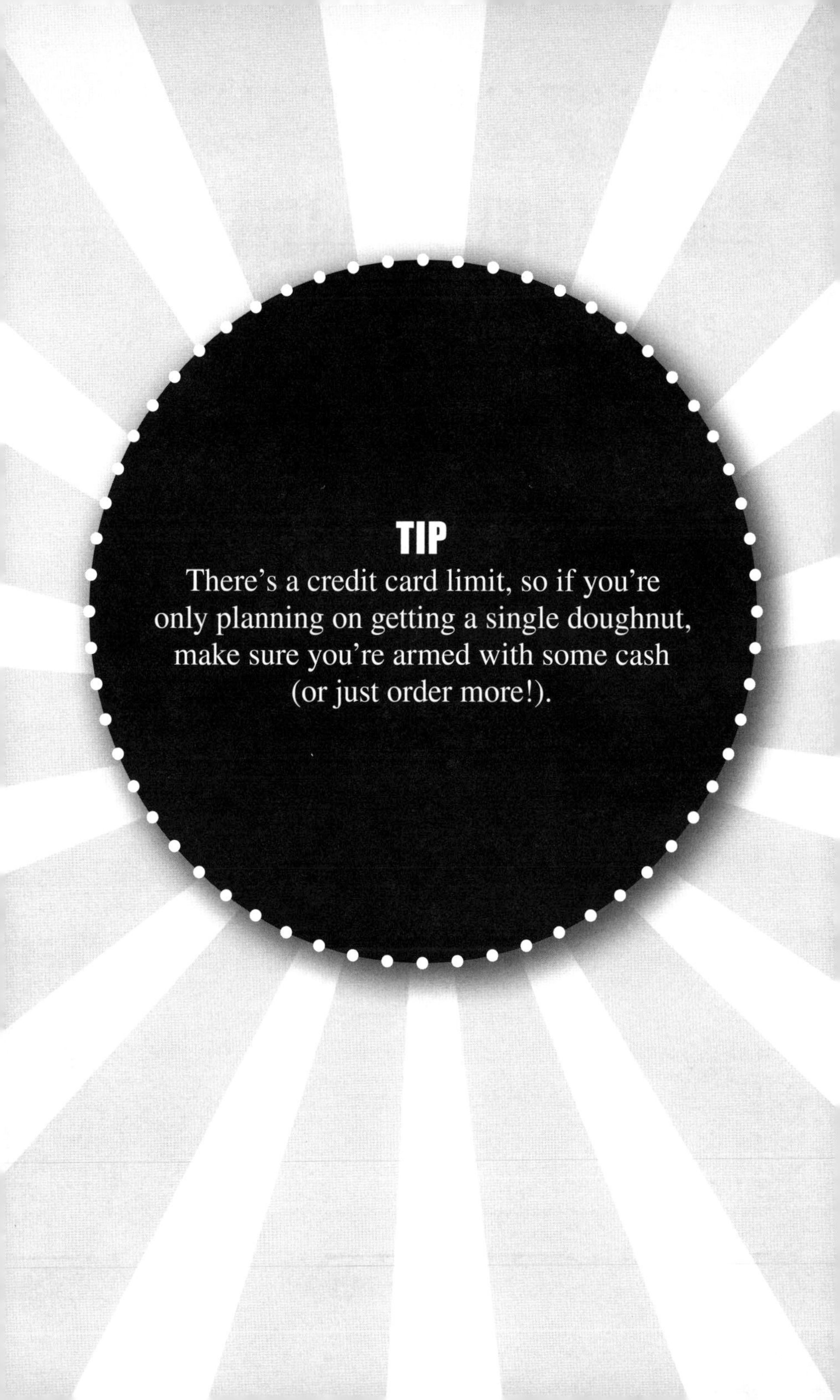

TIP

There's a credit card limit, so if you're only planning on getting a single doughnut, make sure you're armed with some cash (or just order more!).

BE SERVED BRAZILIAN RODIZIO BY GAUCHOS
AT CHIMA

Las Olas Boulevard is a buzzing district filled with restaurants, bars, galleries, and boutiques, but take a drive further east down the boulevard and you'll find Chima. Guests enter a courtyard graced by banyan trees strung with romantic lights, kicking off a night of dining fit for hungry gauchos. The Brazilian cowboys themselves bring 15 rotisserie meats to each table, slicing off decadent pieces of top sirloin, lamb, pork, chicken, sausage, fish, and ribs. On Saturdays, take part in the lunch special that includes seven cuts of meat. With a handful of locations up the east coast of the United States, Fort Lauderdale serves as the flagship location for the Brazilian eatery, where you will never leave hungry.

2400 E Las Olas Blvd., 954-712-0580
chimasteakhouse.com

TIP

Chima offers a bevy of options—including gluten-free dishes—on its menu, so those with food allergies or on a special diet can enjoy Brazilian-style dining, too.

INDULGE IN BRUNCH
AT FOXY BROWN

Brunch is perhaps the most important meal of the week—in Fort Lauderdale, at least. The breakfast and lunch hour menus on Saturdays and Sundays are endless, from loaded latkes, banana bread grilled cheese, chicken 'n waffles sliders, and pancakes with rotating toppings (including Girl Scout Cookies during season) to the crown jewel patty melt that started it all. Besides the standard mimosas and Bloody Marys, the brunchtime cocktail menu includes unique drinks like Luck of the Irish (Jameson and cold brew) or the Hemingway Daiquiri. While brunch is its claim to fame, you can't go wrong with lunch or dinner at the Foxy Brown any other day of the week.

476 N Federal Hwy., 754-200-4236
foxybrownftl.com

TIP

Foxy Brown moved to its new location on Federal Highway in 2021, and in its place on Broward Boulevard is The Katherine, which is also worth a visit.

ORDER A TABLE OF WORLD-FAMOUS GARLIC CRABS
AT THE RUSTIC INN

The Rustic Inn wasn't meant to be a seafood restaurant when it opened in 1955 without a name, but fewer than five years later it would find its destiny. The owner opened up shop as an Italian restaurant and treated himself to some crabs he fished out of the canal. Customers wanted what he was having, and the rest is history—including him getting the restaurant's name by commandeering the neon sign of the Rustic Inn down the road when it closed. They're best known for their garlic crabs, but the menu also includes goodies like fresh oysters, fried alligator, conch salad, Alaskan king crabs and Florida stone crabs (only in season from October 15 to May 1). Crabs are served whole, and customers are handed bibs and crab cracking tools to get to work on their dinner. It's well worth it.

4331 Anglers Ave., 954-842-2804, 954-584-1637
rusticinn.com

GRAB A BEER FROM THE FRIDGE
AT THE RIVERSIDE MARKET

Tucked into a residential area of Riverside Park, the Riverside Market is a farm-store-turned-craft-beer-hangout. Inside, you'll find a wall of refrigerators holding more than 650 types of craft beers hailing from the Sunshine State and beyond. Pick the one you want, grab one of the bottle openers hanging from the ceiling, and bring your empties to the cash register at the end of the night to pay. If you're in the mood to nosh, there's a full menu of snacks, salads, sandwiches, burgers, and pizza. By the way, if you're coming from the north side of the New River, you'll cross over one of the last swing bridges in Fort Lauderdale while driving down 11th Avenue.

608 SW 12th Ave., 954-358-8333
theriversidemarket.com

TIP

The bar has two more locations, one further south in Fort Lauderdale and another in Plantation, plus Tarpon River Brewing.

16

EAT A BURGER BY THE TOILETS
AT LE TUB

OK, so that headline is probably not the most appetizing but hear us out: Le Tub's sirloin burger was once named No. 1 in the top 20 burgers you need to eat before you die by *GQ* magazine. Le Tub has humble beginnings: the owner converted a Sunoco gas station into a restaurant in 1974. Over the years it's collected eclectic decor, including its iconic painted toilet bowls, bathtubs filled with flowers and greenery, old signage, life preservers, and buoys. The multi-level, outdoor diner is hidden behind greenery right off A1A on the Intracoastal in Hollywood, but we just let you in on the secret. While you're there, add the seafood gumbo and Key lime pie to the order for a well-rounded meal.

Le Tub
1100 N Ocean Dr., Hollywood, 954-921-9425
theletub.com

17

PIG OUT ON BRAZILIAN FOOD IN THE BACKYARD
OF REGINA'S FARM

If you've ever wanted a home-cooked meal in the abode of a new friend, then make a reservation for the next dinner at Regina's Farm. An urban farm in the heart of Fort Lauderdale, Regina welcomes the public to her backyard to dine buffet style on hearty plates of polenta, chicken, beef, rice, vegetables, soups, desserts, and her famous cheese bread, or *pão de queijo*. While waiting to eat, you'll see kids riding a tractor, hear chickens clucking, and inhale the heavenly smells of dinner coming from the brick stove. Once Regina announces that the meal is ready to eat, everyone sits together at picnic tables. South Florida might be known for quick outbursts of rain, but Regina and her family will usher guests into their living room to wait out the storm. It doesn't get more family style than this.

1101 Middle St., 954-465-1900
reginasfarm.com

TIP

Dinner at Regina's Farm books up months in advance, so right after you book your tickets to Fort Lauderdale, text to make a reservation.

TASTE THE RAINBOW
AT CYTH & CO

This might be a coffee shop, but it's an all-day affair at Cyth & Co. Located in the growing downtown Oakland Park neighborhood, customers can come for a cup of joe or venture into the colorful side of the menu, like the baby blue Butterfly Latte, frothy pink Blush Crush, or berry hibiscus kombucha. Nosh on their all-day breakfast and lunch menu or peruse seasonal specials and sweet treats from the bakery like guava and cheese empanada, coffee crumb cake or chocolate cookies. Cyth & Co. also mixes things up for holidays big and small with limited edition drinks like lattes made with pink or green mocha syrups. The shop serves as a place of inspiration, swathed in moody floral wallpaper and art deco decor, with a focal point on the golden coffee bar and bright green La Marzocco espresso maker. So come for your daily caffeine kick, snag a table to get some work done, or order a cocktail during happy hour with a friend. Be sure to check them out on social media for pop up events.

3446 NE 12th Ave., Oakland Park, 954-999-0662
cythco.com

OTHER COFFEE SHOPS WORTH A VISIT IN THE FORT LAUDERDALE AREA

Wells Coffee Co.
737 NE 2nd Ave., 954-982-2886
599 SW 2nd Ave.
wellscoffees.com

Circle House Coffee
727 NE 3rd Ave., Ste. #100, 954-870-6456
119 W Oakland Park Blvd., Oakland Park
circlehousecoffee.com

Undergrounds Coffeehaus
3020 N Federal Hwy., Ste. 5A, 954-630-1900
facebook.com/undergrounds.coffeehaus

HAVE DINNER ON A GONDOLA

WITH RIVERFRONT GONDOLA TOURS

You don't have to fly to Venice to enjoy a gondola ride, not when there's the Venice of America right here in Florida. Riverfront Gondola Tours organizes 90-minute rides through the heart of Fort Lauderdale on the New River—either with friends or that special someone—cruising through the city's river and canal system. Gondoliers will share details of the city's history, an up-close view of the mega-yachts, and scoops on the waterfront mansions and the many celebrities who have called Fort Lauderdale home. Guests are welcome to bring their own food and drink, but the company has a special partnership with downtown waterfront restaurant Casa Sensei that allows customers to order dinner ahead of time to enjoy during the ride. The menu is a collection of Latin American and Asian fusion dishes, including an extensive sushi and raw menu. The electric gondolas can carry a maximum of six people, not including the gondolier.

1200 E Las Olas Blvd., 954-616-7699
riverfrontgondolatours.com

EAT DINNER NEXT TO SOPHIA LOREN
AT SEA WATCH

With three acres of beach and floor-to-ceiling windows, there are no bad views at Sea Watch. The beachside seafood restaurant welcomes guests through its solid wood door, with a porthole revealing an old-school restaurant with wood and brick interior. On the walls are black-and-white photos of celebrities from yesteryear, including Marilyn Monroe, Marlon Brando, Rosemary Clooney, and Sophia Loren. They'll keep you company as you enjoy a bottle of wine and classic dishes like oysters, lobster bisque, blackened mahi mahi, seared scallops, and pasta. For the best views, ask to sit on the second floor to watch the moon rise over the Atlantic Ocean and the palm trees sway in the wind.

6002 N Ocean Blvd., 954-781-2200
seawatchontheocean.com

DINE IN A LANDMARK

AT THE HISTORIC DOWNTOWNER

Locals have been going to The Historic Downtowner for decades, where laid-back dining goes hand-in-hand with riverfront views. Come out for brunch, trivia nights, and live music; order a drink and a meal or snack at the long wooden bar while watching a game; or watch the Water Taxis come in. The large menu includes bar favorites like tacos and sandwiches, as well as dishes you'll only find locally, like dolphin fingers, Tericado mahi, and Key lime pie. The building's origins date back to the 1920s when it was Maxwell's Arcade. It survived the Great Miami Hurricane of 1926 (a dark landmark in South Florida history) and The Downtowner stepped in later to carry on the legacy of the Mediterranean Revival structure to become a Fort Lauderdale gem. While its indoor AC is a big draw, there are also spots for sitting outside on the seawall steps away from the New River, as well as sidewalk seating. Also on the property is the aptly named, brick-laden Maxwell Room, which is set up for private events.

10 S New River Dr. E, 954-463-9800
thehistoricdowntowner.com

TAKE A TRIP THROUGH POLYNESIA
AT THE MAI-KAI

There are plenty of iconic restaurants in Fort Lauderdale, but none pack a punch as much as the Mai-Kai Polynesian restaurant. For starters, you can't miss it as you're driving down US-1, with its soaring palm trees, tiki huts, torches, and rock landscaping that'll have you feeling like you're entering another world. Schedule dinner and a show complete with hula and fire dancers, musicians, dishes that are pleasing to both the eye and the palate, and plenty of tropical drinks. The landmark restaurant, which was opened in 1956 by the Thornton family, experienced major flooding damage in 2020. Thankfully, investors swooped in to renovate the icon while maintaining the allure that made it *Coastal Living* magazine's best tiki bar in the United States and an addition to the National Register of Historic Places.

3599 N Federal Hwy., 954-563-3272
maikai.com

EAT YOUR WAY
ALONG LAS OLAS BOULEVARD

With so many restaurants on Las Olas Boulevard, the district could probably have its own book on places to eat before you die. The boulevard is one of the biggest attractions in downtown Fort Lauderdale, a gathering place for special events as well as a day-to-day place to be for people-watching and dining. Indulge in Italian food in the courtyard of Louie Bossi, where you can also play a round of bocce ball; browse the extensive list of tequilas and mezcals at El Camino; get your fill of classic American food at Big City Tavern; pour your own brew at American Social, where there are beer taps right at your table—and we're just getting started. Savor the empanadas at Argentino Las Olas, seafood towers at Wild Sea Oyster Bar, tikka masala at Bombay Darbar, lamb meatballs at Ya Mas . . . from brunch and lunch to dinner or a nightcap, whatever you're craving you're likely to find it on Las Olas Boulevard.

lasolasboulevard.com

GET A TASTE OF LAS OLAS
WITH CRAFT FOOD TOURS

The dining options in Fort Lauderdale may seem endless, and that's because they are. When you're pressed for time, opt for a smorgasbord of downtown Fort Lauderdale's restaurant scene with Craft Food Tours. Scheduled only on Saturdays, the three-hour guided walking tours include four seated tastings at restaurants located on Las Olas Boulevard, adding up to eight or more dishes and three alcoholic beverages. Not only will you get to try the food, but the tours also include chats with the staff and chefs at the restaurants who participate in Craft Food Tours; these include Wild Sea, El Camino, Cuba Libre, B Square, Argentino, and Ann's Florist.

craftfoodtours.com

TIP

Craft Food Tours got its start in another foodie city, Delray Beach, about 35 minutes north of Fort Lauderdale.

Friday Night Sound Waves in Fort Lauderdale

MUSIC AND ENTERTAINMENT

25

GET DINNER WITH A SIDE OF DRAG
AT LIPS

Join the gaggles of birthday and bachelorette parties on their way to Lips, a favorite for drag shows in Fort Lauderdale. With big hair, sky-high heels, over-the-top costumes, and plenty of good-hearted jokes, you're in for a great time with the area's best drag queens. There's also celebrity impersonators, for divas such as Cher and Beyoncé, who aren't just stunning lookalikes but can belt it, too! The ladies of Lips host themed shows five nights a week, from Wednesday-night Bingo and performances by musical divas to their infamous Gospel Brunch on Sunday mornings. There are dinner and show packages available, while some shows have a required minimum at the bar or from the menu. With multiple shows on Fridays and Saturdays, the later you attend, the raunchier the show will be.

1421 E Oakland Park Blvd., 954-567-0987
fladragshow.com

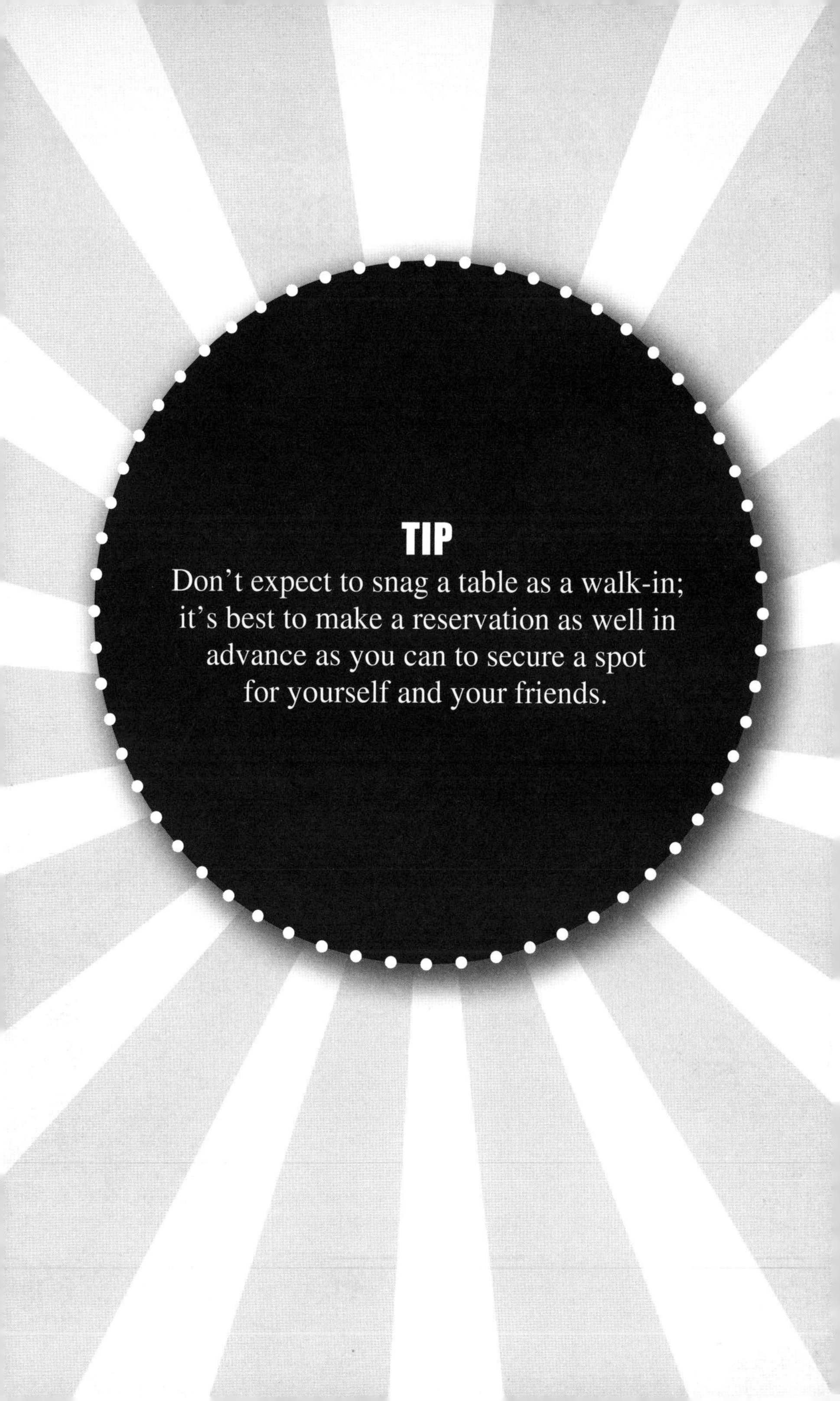

TIP

Don't expect to snag a table as a walk-in; it's best to make a reservation as well in advance as you can to secure a spot for yourself and your friends.

DANCE TO COUNTRY MUSIC
AT TORTUGA MUSIC FESTIVAL

With the arrival of spring in Fort Lauderdale comes one of the most highly anticipated music festivals in the area—the Tortuga Music Festival. The three-day fête on Fort Lauderdale Beach draws top country music artists to its multiple stages, with high-caliber headliners like Tim McGraw, Miranda Lambert, Luke Bryan, Kenny Chesney, Zac Brown Band, and Morgan Wallen. Musical acts from other genres are added to the mix as well. Between sets, concert-goers can explore the Conservation Village with activities and entertainment, as well as grab a bite to eat from food trucks using eco-friendly materials. Each year, Tortuga Music Festival benefits Rock the Ocean, a charity that promotes turtle and shark conservation, coral reef protection, reversing overfishing, and other marine initiatives.

tortugamusicfestival.com

MARVEL AT THE AERIAL DAREDEVILS

DURING THE FORT LAUDERDALE AIR SHOW

Each spring, Fort Lauderdale's skies light up with the exciting performances of military airplanes and daredevil pilots. It's the Fort Lauderdale Air Show, where acts such as the Air Force Thunderbirds and performers from Red Bull whiz over Fort Lauderdale Beach in death-defying acts. Think: group formations, narrowly missing each other while performing barrel rolls, and daring jump patterns. The show offers ticketed seats on the beach as well as VIP seating on hotel terraces, and restaurants, bars, and hotels also get in on the action with viewing parties of their own. If you have access to a boat, set out to sea (there are open areas designated by the Coast Guard) and watch the planes from the Atlantic Ocean. Plus, the day before the show is the "dress rehearsal," so you can always get a sneak peek of the action before the big day.

fortlauderdaleairshow.com

TIP

Avoid the traffic and parking troubles by riding the Water Taxi to the beach from downtown.

GET INTO THE PIT
AT REVOLUTION LIVE

This is no place to sit and golf clap to musical acts. Since 2004, Revolution Live on downtown Fort Lauderdale's Himmarshee Street has been a standing-only venue, giving concert-goers the chance to get up close and personal with the bands on stage. If you don't enjoy the pit crush, head to the second-floor mezzanine to watch the local bands or touring performers from up high. If the scene at Revolution Live looks familiar, you may recognize it from the movie *Rock of Ages*—starring Tom Cruise and Alec Baldwin—where it served as the Bourbon Room for the film, and the prop bras are still hanging over the bar. When staff isn't setting up or breaking down a show, Revolution Live also takes part in community events, such as hosting the Indie Craft Bazaar.

100 SW 3rd Ave., 954-449-1025
jointherevolution.net

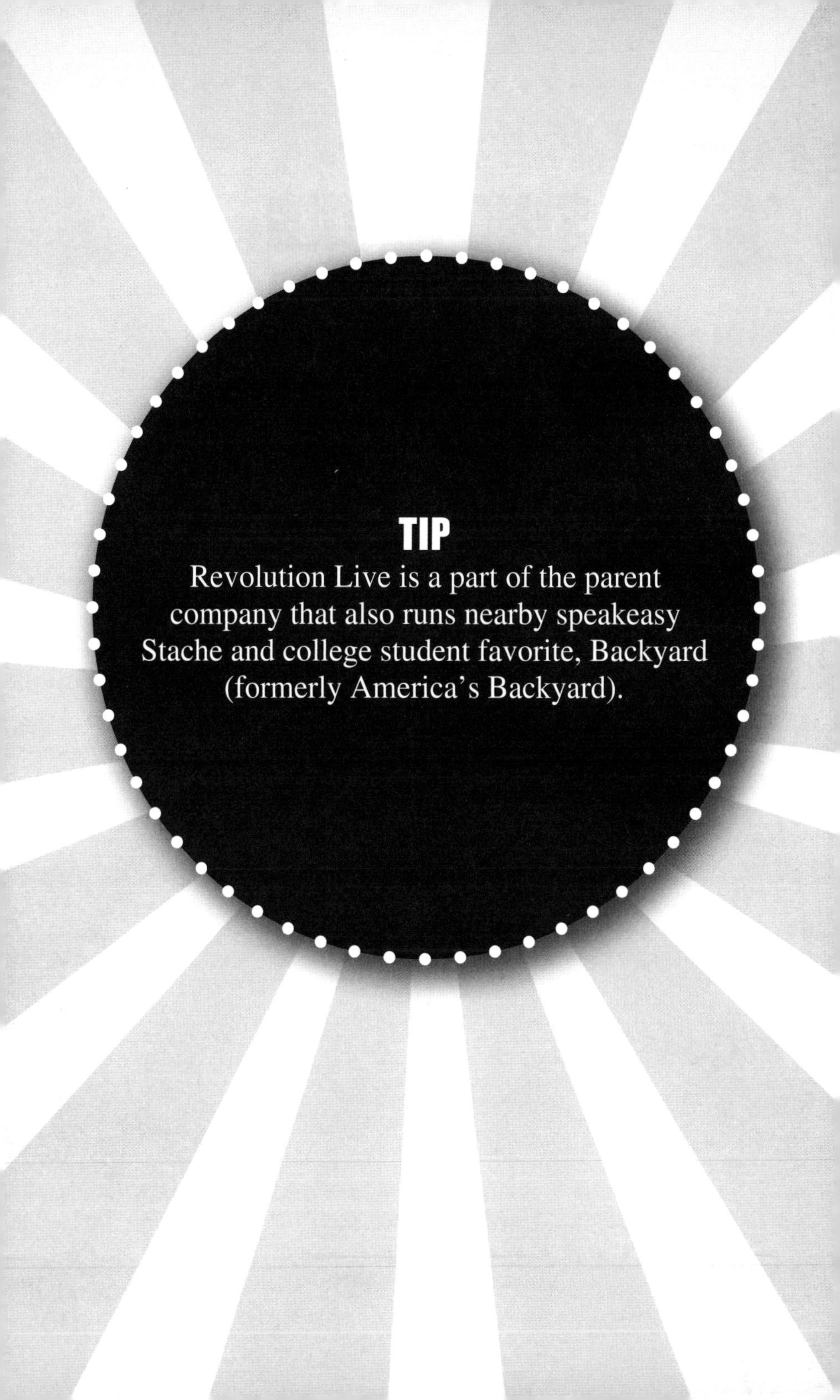

TIP

Revolution Live is a part of the parent company that also runs nearby speakeasy Stache and college student favorite, Backyard (formerly America's Backyard).

SING ALONG TO A MUSICAL
AT THE BROWARD CENTER

From *Hamilton* to *Cats*, ballets to comedy, and orchestras to popular speakers, some of the greatest performers and shows in the country have graced the stage at the Broward Center for the Performing Arts. The theater seats more than 2,600 people from the upper balcony to lower orchestra, but given its impeccable lighting and acoustics, every single guest will enjoy the show. The Broward Center is situated in the downtown district of Himmarshee Street, meaning ticket holders can get dinner at restaurants like Pizza Craft (walk all the way to the back to enter the speakeasy Apothecary 330) before walking over to the Broward Center for the show. In addition, patrons can get a drink at the center's Intermezzo Lounge or theater's lobby. Just make sure you're there when the bells ring to find your seats!

201 SW 5th Ave., 954-462-0222
browardcenter.org

WATCH A SHOW AND SEE THE NEW DIGS

AT THE PARKER

More intimate than the Broward Center but nonetheless a stellar theater, The Parker's classic red curtain has kicked off many performances since its opening night in 1967. The Neoclassical performing arts center underwent an impressive $25 million renovation and was rebranded as The Parker in 2021. Now, guests can indulge in drinks and snacks at Bernie Peck's Bar in the lobby, manned by 12 bartenders. Or, when buying your ticket, spring for the VIP experience at The Haller Club during the hour before the show and later, at intermission, offering gratis soft drinks, premium beer and wine, coffee, tea, and hors d'oeuvres, as well as cocktails at lower prices than those found in the lobby.

707 NE 8th St., 954-462-0222
parkerplayhouse.com

FOLLOW THE TUNES
TO BLUE JEAN BLUES

Blaring saxophones and soothing, soulful voices make jazz a way of life at Blue Jean Blues; hence their scheduling of live performances seven days a week. The vibe changes each night, with the crowd getting up on its feet to some funky beat one day or sitting at the bar listening to moody, pensive blues tunes the next. Also, there is a happy hour celebration every day from 4 to 7 p.m., and guests can order from a full dinner menu that includes an impressive list of pizza choices. The owners sometimes plan alfresco shows, so you can enjoy bluesy crooning just blocks away from Fort Lauderdale Beach. As Blue Jean Blues is an intimate setting, it's best to make reservations to ensure a table for you and your group.

3320 NE 33rd St., 954-306-6330
bluejeanblues.live

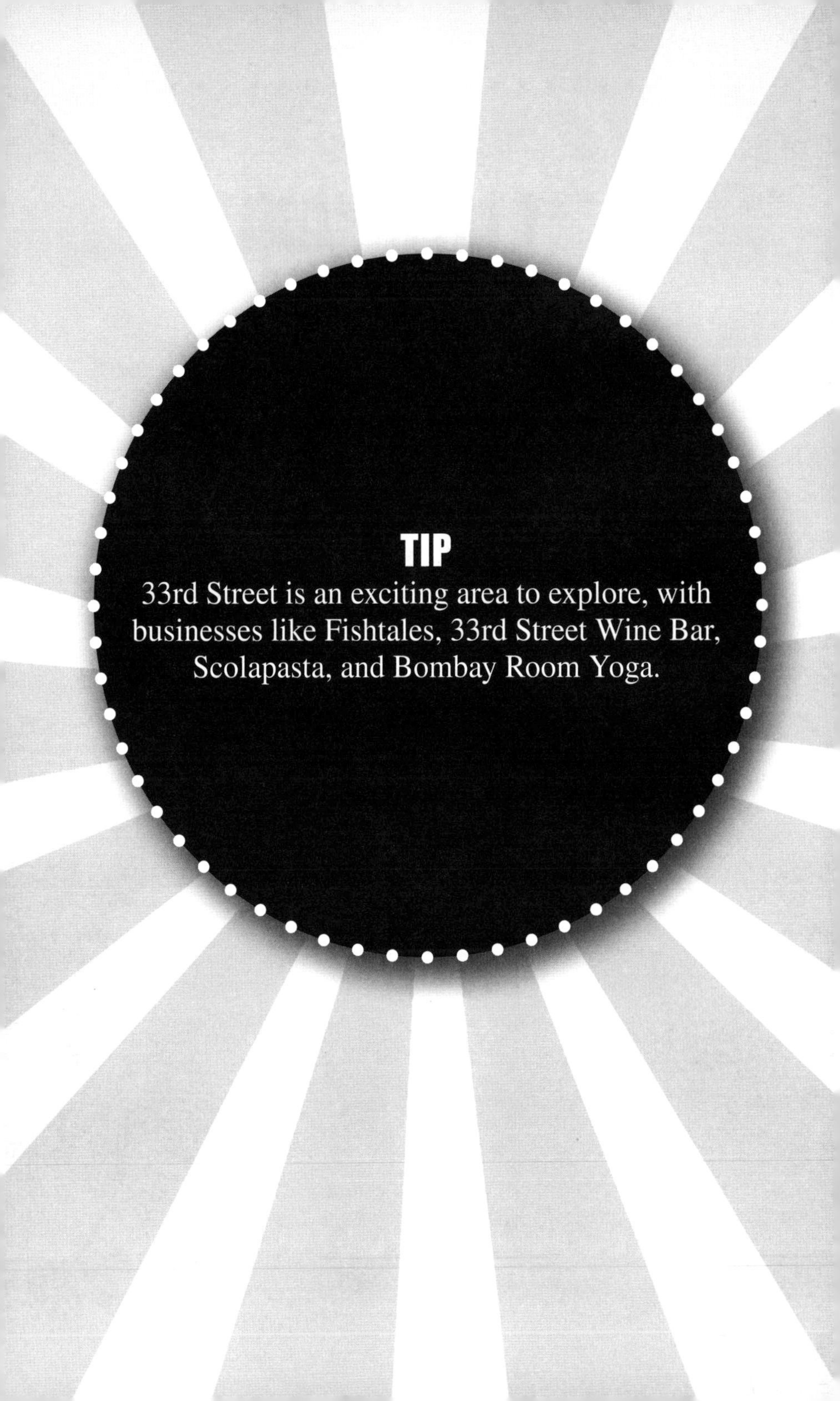

TIP

33rd Street is an exciting area to explore, with businesses like Fishtales, 33rd Street Wine Bar, Scolapasta, and Bombay Room Yoga.

MEET MERMAIDS
AT THE WRECK BAR

Mermaids aren't just in fairy tales; they come to life at the B Ocean Resort's Wreck Bar. In this cozy bar, the wall is a series of portholes from the hotel's peekaboo swimming pool for aquatic shows. The hotel was built in 1956 and was originally named the Yankee Clipper, drawing the likes of Marilyn Monroe and Joe DiMaggio to the mermaid shows and the Polynesian Room on the second floor. In fact, the bar was one of the backdrops for the film *Analyze This* with Robert De Niro and Billy Crystal. Each week, mermaids perform in the Coral Reef Mermaid Show for kids, Mermaids and Mimosas for Sunday brunch, and an evening burlesque show with mermaids and aquamen. In 2022, the Wreck Bar brought back the tiki theme in the Polynesian Room, complete with hula dancing and island tunes.

1140 Seabreeze Blvd., 954-245-3836
bhotelsandresorts.com

33

GET YOUR SWEAT ON WITH THE BANDS

AT THE CULTURE ROOM

There's no shortage of live music venues in Fort Lauderdale, but Culture Room has had staying power for its intimate crowd experience. With a roster of up-and-coming indie acts to nationally recognized rappers and rock bands, the standing-room-only venue is a place to cross off concerts on your "to see" list. With general admission tickets, visitors can arrive early (but not too early, no more than an hour) to ensure a spot on the balcony or floor. Culture Room is an unassuming club located in a strip mall with neighbors like a tattoo shop, Irish pub, and Chinese restaurant, but don't let that fool you. Step inside and you're transported to a place where it's just you, the band, and about 600 fellow fans.

3045 N Federal Hwy., #60-E, 954-564-1074
cultureroom.net

COME FACE TO FACE WITH LARGE REPTILES
AT GATOR BOYS ALLIGATOR RESCUE

You might recognize the Gator Boys from the *Animal Planet* TV show, and you can see them up close and personal with these ancient creatures: alligators. The rescue area is located inside Everglades Holiday Park, which more than 200,000 alligators call home—as natural inhabitants or ones that have been rescued from backyards, swimming pools, and garages, among other places. At the park, guests can learn facts about the reptiles, hold baby gators, and watch a family-friendly alligator wrestling show in the "Gator Pit." The sport descends from and was popularized by the Seminole and Miccosukee tribes, with tricks like pinning an alligator's mouth back with the wrestler's chin, giving it a kiss, and the "Florida smile," or making the alligator open its mouth with the wrestler's hands.

21940 Griffin Rd., 954-434-8111
evergladesholidaypark.com/gators

BEAT THE SUNDAY SCARIES

AT SUNDAY JAZZ BRUNCH

With sunny days for most of the year, Fort Lauderdale likes to spend its weekends outside. During the first Sunday of the month, the city organizes a free Sunday Jazz Brunch complete with jazz bands performing on three stages from 11 a.m. to 2 p.m. Performers range from local bands of all genres to the Florida Atlantic University Jazz Orchestra and US Navy Jazz & Brass Bands. The event is set in Esplanade Park in the downtown Riverfront, making for an enjoyable afternoon by the New River. Bring a chair and picnic blanket to listen to the tunes by the gazebo or stages, or walk with friends and family (including dogs) to explore the Riverwalk with the sounds of jazz wafting in the breeze.

400 SW 2nd St., 954-828-5363
parks.fortlauderdale.gov/special-events/special-events/jazz-brunch

TIP

Esplanade Park is just steps away from the Broward Center, the Museum of Discovery and Science, and a variety of restaurants like Rivertail, the Wharf, and the stretch of Himmarshee Street.

EXPERIENCE AN IMMERSIVE SHOW

AT THE FOUNDRY AND ISLAND CITY STAGE

Wilton Manors, or "the gayborhood," has developed its own independent theater scene, thanks to productions coming out of The Foundry and Island City Stage. The neighboring theater companies produce plays and musicals all year long, leading to multiple Carbonell Awards for both. Local playwright Ronnie Larsen founded Plays of Wilton (POW!) at The Foundry to encourage theater arts in the community, and he regularly puts on boundary-pushing LGBTQ-themed plays that get people talking. Island City Stage also puts on plays focusing on the community, both by locals and lauded masters like Tennessee Williams. Theater troupe Infinite Abyss also uses the stage, exploring darker themes with productions focusing on horror, suspense, and gothic dramas (here, Valentine's Day is Dracula Day!). The stages are located on buzzing Wilton Drive, where ticket holders can dine at nearby trendy restaurants before enjoying the show.

TIP

Parking places are tough to come by, so arrive early or consider using a rideshare service.

2306 N Dixie Hwy., Wilton Manors, 954-826-8790
ronnielarsen.com

Island City Stage
2304 N Dixie Hwy., Wilton Manors, 954-928-9800
islandcitystage.org

EAT, SHOP, AND JAM
AT SISTRUNK MARKET & BREWERY

Food halls have made their mark in South Florida, and Fort Lauderdale has its very own Sistrunk Market & Brewery. Here, you can grab a table, use the QR code to order from any of a dozen vendors, and have your food brought to you—but it's so much more than a food hall. Foodies can take part in pairing dinners, cocktail tastings, pizza-making classes, and tours of the brewery and distillery. For those who love the performing arts, there's live music from Thursday to Sunday, DJs playing in the hidden rum lounge, comedy shows, and even music production courses. Finally, the Kollective Shop inside the marketplace sells artwork, handmade soaps, jewelry, and other goodies. Like we said, it's way more than a food hall.

115 NW 6th St., 954-329-2551
sistrunkmarketplace.com

TIP

There's limited free parking, so be prepared to pay in the overflow lot.

WATCH IT SNOW IN FORT LAUDERDALE

AT CHRISTMAS ON LAS OLAS

Each year, South Florida commemorates the time it snowed in Miami in 1977. But locals don't have to bundle up or wait for the anomaly to happen again, thanks to the decades-old tradition of Christmas on Las Olas. Since 1962, the boulevard has been transformed into a winter wonderland with local children's choirs, vendors, artisans, Christmas trees, and lights all along the boulevard, and an "ice" skating rink with "snow" gently falling over the crowd. The free event is scheduled for the end of November each year, kicking off the holiday season with a local flair you can only find in Fort Lauderdale. Perhaps the best part is that the fun event benefits local nonprofits, like the Florida Children's Theatre, Broward Center, the Rotary Club of Fort Lauderdale, Miami City Ballet, and more.

Las Olas Blvd.
lasolasboulevard.com/christmasonlasolas

WAIT FOR SANTA'S YACHT
AT THE WINTERFEST BOAT PARADE

An age-old Fort Lauderdale tradition, the Winterfest Boat Parade has exploded over the decades from a few guys drinking beers on the river to the "Biggest Show on H20." Locals vie for tickets to get a seat in VIP viewing areas, gather at homes located on the New River and Intracoastal, or lay down a picnic blanket to watch from the riverbank. The 12-mile route takes a parade of boats—decorated to reflect the year's theme—from the Stranahan House, up the Intracoastal to Pompano Beach, and back down to the Broward Center. Multiple events kick off the Winterfest Boat Parade, including the elaborate Black Tie Ball at the Seminole Hard Rock Hotel & Casino, family fun day, and the event poster debut. A celebrity grand marshal is chosen each year, with the likes of Kim Kardashian, Joan Rivers, Dan Marino, Regis Philbin, Pitbull, Flo Rida, and others taking the helm to emcee the parade. The event has also expanded beyond Fort Lauderdale: in recent years it has been televised up the eastern seaboard and viewed by millions online and on TV.

New River and Intracoastal Waterway
winterfestparade.com

SING ALONG TO *ROCKY HORROR PICTURE SHOW*
AT GATEWAY CINEMA

One of the most enduring historical landmarks in Fort Lauderdale is the Gateway Cinema "at the bend" of Federal Highway, identifiable by its movie marquee from yesteryear. Its first film screening was *Up Front* back in 1951, and today movie fans can watch new blockbusters, indie flicks, and art films in one of the theater's four auditoriums. An ongoing tradition at the Gateway is a monthly screening of rock opera *Rocky Horror Picture Show*, complete with a collaborative show by shadow cast The Faithful Handymen. The acting troupe sells survival packs before each show, filled with props to use throughout the theatrical experiences. Each year, the movie theater is also one of three theaters in Fort Lauderdale and Hollywood to host the Fort Lauderdale International Film Festival (FLIFF).

1820 E Sunrise Blvd., 954-278-8966
fliff.com/gateway

41

DANCE TO THE BANDS
AT FRIDAY NIGHT SOUND WAVES

Thank God It's Friday! End the week with free concerts at Las Olas Oceanside Park (also known as the LOOP) with area bands of all genres. Located across the street from Fort Lauderdale Beach, attendees can bring picnic blankets and chairs from which to enjoy the tunes all night long. Before the bands take the stage, patrons can enjoy the makers market, food vendors, fitness classes, and other activities. Families with school-aged children can also take part in the CATCH Kids Club for activities centered around health and physical activity. Programming for Friday Night Sound Waves runs from mid-March to the Fourth of July weekend, then picks up again in October through the end of the year. There are also bonus performances on Christmas Eve and New Year's Eve.

3000 E Las Olas Blvd.
fridaynightsoundwaves.com

SING ALONG WITH 20,000 NEW FRIENDS
AT THE FLA LIVE ARENA

When the biggest musical acts make their way to Broward County, they're sure to have a show (or two) at the FLA Live Arena. It's also the home of the Florida Panthers hockey team, meaning that the area also plays host to ice shows, including Disney on Ice. The arena boasts almost 21,000 seats for fans of everyone from rockers and rappers to acrobats and ice skaters. It's also across the street from the Sawgrass Mills Mall, a popular spot to meet up for drinks or dinner before walking over to the FLA Live Arena for the show.

1 Panther Pkwy., Sunrise, 954-835-7000
flalivearena.com

TIP

The arena underwent a name change in 2021, so you may hear locals still refer to it as the BB&T Center (or even its predecessor, the BankAtlantic Center).

GULP DOWN A TANKARD OF ALE
AT THE FLORIDA RENAISSANCE FESTIVAL

Head to Quiet Waters Park as a citizen of the 21st century, but once you enter the gate, you become a member of the 16th century village of Kimmendale. For more than a month each year, the Florida Renaissance Festival takes over the park with jousting, sword fights, minstrels, an artisan marketplace, carnival rides, food fit for royalty, and plenty of ale to keep your tankard full. Three times a day, brave knights mount their steeds for a joust to the death while crowds cheer on their favorites from the stands. Throughout the marketplace, merchants hawk their wares of hand-blown glass, themed clothing, leatherworking, carved wood figures, and other crafts. There's always something different when you attend the Renaissance Festival, because each weekend has its own special theme. But no matter when you go, you're in for a great time. Huzzah!

401 S Powerline Rd., Deerfield Beach, 954-776-1642
ren-fest.com

WASTE AWAY (AGAIN)
AT THE MARGARITAVILLE BEACH RESORT

You don't have to make the drive to Key West to tap into the lifestyle, thanks to Margaritaville in Hollywood. Yes, an entire resort dedicated to Jimmy Buffet's catalog of music exists, including a giant statue of a busted flip flop. With eight restaurants and grills, it's going to take a few trips to taste test each location. But best of all is the entertainment schedule lined up at Margaritaville, with live music Thursdays through Sundays at Jimmy Buffett's Margaritaville Restaurant, and Wednesdays through Sundays at both the 5 O'Clock Somewhere Bar & Grill and the Hollywood Beach Bandshell. Bands cover a plethora of genres like rock, country, Top 40, reggae, and Latin, making for a night that'll leave you happier than a "Cheeseburger in Paradise."

1111 N Ocean Dr., Hollywood, 954-874-4444
margaritavillehollywoodbeachresort.com

45

TAP INTO YOUR INNER BULL RIDER
AT THE BERGERON RODEO GROUNDS

When most people think of Florida, they conjure images of the Sunshine State's idyllic beaches and prehistoric alligators. But what they may not know is that Florida has a rich cowboy and rodeo history. In the town of Davie, west of Fort Lauderdale, rodeos are scheduled multiple times a year at the Bergeron Rodeo Grounds. It's located in the town's western-themed downtown and includes a 72,000-square-foot arena that seats 5,500 people. The first rodeo was hosted in the town in 1946, and in 1986, the Weekley and Parrish families teamed up to host Professional Rodeo Cowboys Association-sanctioned rodeos. Today, there are youth and adult rodeo competitions, including the Orange Blossom Festival Rodeo and the highly anticipated Southeastern Circuit Finals Rodeo.

4271 Davie Rd., Davie, 954-680-8005
davieprorodeo.com

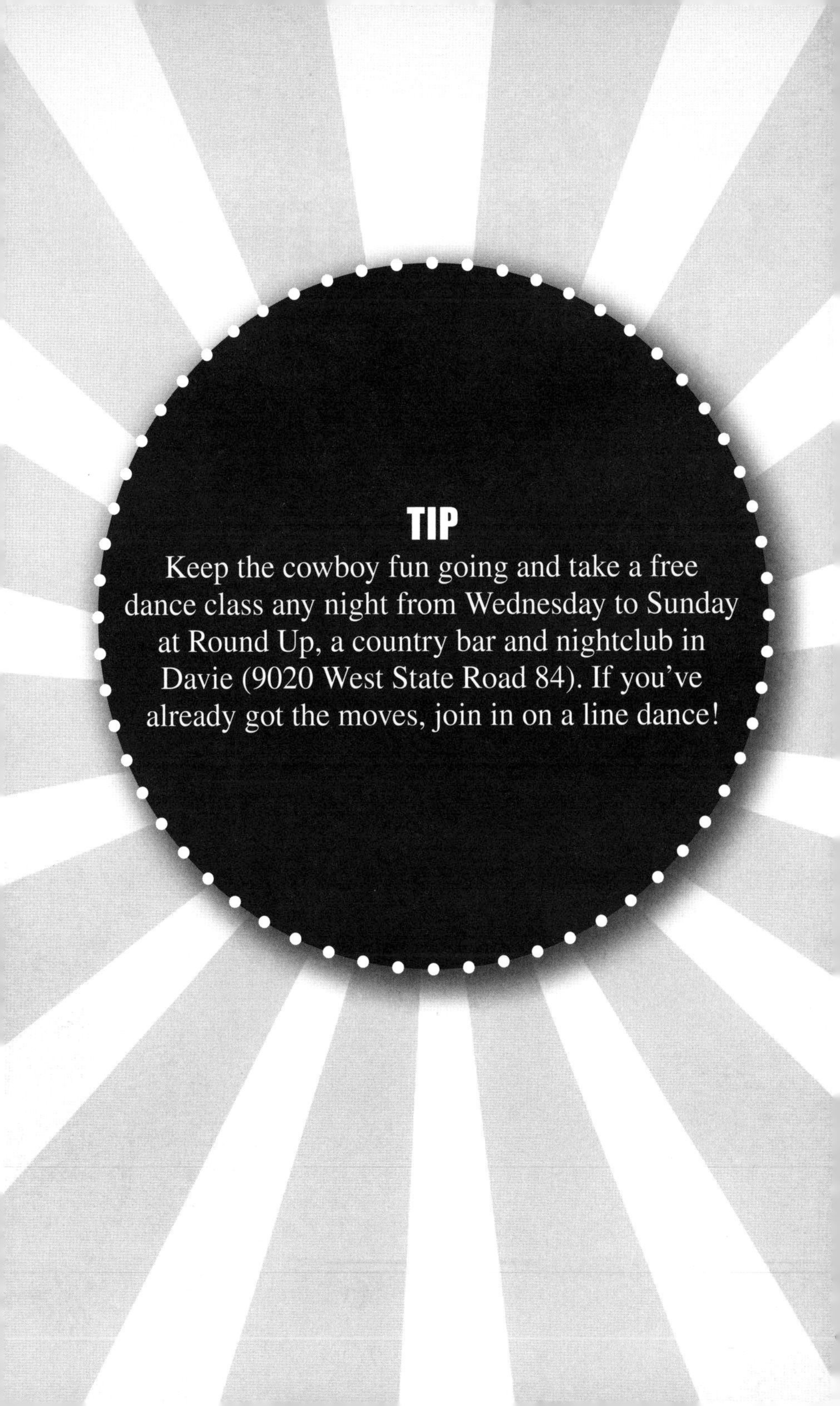

TIP

Keep the cowboy fun going and take a free dance class any night from Wednesday to Sunday at Round Up, a country bar and nightclub in Davie (9020 West State Road 84). If you've already got the moves, join in on a line dance!

WATCH FILMS FROM AROUND THE WORLD
AT THE FORT LAUDERDALE INTERNATIONAL FILM FESTIVAL

Cinephiles are in for a treat every winter when local theaters take part in the Fort Lauderdale International Film Festival, or FLIFF. Over the course of the week, hundreds of films are screened from those made by on-the-rise filmmakers to Oscar-winning movies, as well as foreign and independent films. During the festival, interviews and seminars are hosted, as well as parties where guests can meet directors and actors from their new favorite film. Participating theaters are Savor Cinema and Gateway Cinema in Fort Lauderdale, and Cinema Paradiso in Hollywood. When the movie marathon is over, though, don't worry: throughout the year there are special events such as movies on a boat or dinner-and-a-movie gatherings.

fliff.org

TASTE TEST CHILI
AT THE 99.9 KISS COUNTRY CHILI COOKOFF

Put on your cowboy boots and Stetsons and bring your taste testing spoon for the annual 99.9 Kiss Country Chili Cookoff. Hosted each January at CB Park in Pembroke Pines, the all-day affair brings together the cowboy meal with country tunes. For the price of a ticket, attendees get to see some of the biggest country music acts on the airwaves—past performers include Garth Brooks, Brad Paisley, Luke Combs, and The Chicks—all the while indulging in various forms of delicious chili. Chefs competing in the contest can enter two categories, traditional red and homestyle chili, and there are also other food vendors providing other food and drink options to keep you fueled throughout the festival.

audacy.com/wkis

TIP

Parking fees are not included in the ticket price, so stuff as many friends as you can into your vehicle!

The Florida Panthers take the ice.
Photo courtesy of Anthony J Rayburn, anthonyjrayburn.com

SPORTS AND RECREATION

48

RENT A BEACH CHAIR AND UMBRELLA
AT FORT LAUDERDALE BEACH

What is a trip to Fort Lauderdale without a visit to the beach? Whether you want to soak up the sun on a beach towel, ride a rental bike along A1A, swim in the ocean, jet ski, or pick up a game of volleyball, the long stretch of beach is filled with oceanside activities. A1A runs along the sandy stretch of Fort Lauderdale Beach, separating the beach from the hotels, restaurants, and bars on the other side, but there are plenty of crosswalks as well as a few pedestrian bridges connecting to hotels (however, you must be a guest to use them). Guests at these hotels can also opt to do chair rentals, although there are companies offering rentals to anyone looking for a day on the sand.

myfortlauderdalebeach.com

SEE THE GUITAR HOTEL LIGHT UP
AT THE SEMINOLE HARD ROCK HOTEL & CASINO

Flying into the Fort Lauderdale-Hollywood International Airport at night, travelers can't help but notice a brightly lit purple guitar in the distance. It's the Guitar Hotel, a part of the newly reimagined Seminole Hard Rock Hotel & Casino in Hollywood, which underwent a $1.5 billion upgrade. The hotel is even more impressive on site, coupled with fountains and a light show each evening. There's something for everyone at the Hard Rock, from slot machines and blackjack tables to fine dining at restaurants like Abiaka and Council Oak, as well as parties at the indoor-outdoor nightclub DAER. Scattered throughout the space are displays of costumes and clothing worn by famous performers including Cher, Jennifer Lopez, Michael Jackson, Madonna, and more. Check the calendar before you go, as the venue also plays host to comedy shows and musicians throughout the year.

1 Seminole Way, Hollywood, 866-502-7529
seminolehardrockhollywood.com

PADDLE UNDER THE MOONLIGHT

WITH FULL MOON KAYAK TOURS

Florida's waterways are a sight to see during the day, but they present a whole other world once the sun sets. Take off on a kayak at Hugh Taylor Birch State Park for one of its monthly Full Moon Kayak Tours, armed with solar-powered lights to lead the way through the park's coastal dune lake, an endangered ecosystem. Scheduled during the full moon, the 45-minute guided tour gives participants a chance to see the mangroves and wildlife literally in a different light. Participants also have the option to do the tour atop a paddleboard. Done in partnership with the park's restaurant, Park & Ocean, close out the night with a campfire and snacks.

Full Moon Kayak Tours
3109 E Sunrise Blvd., 954-357-2610
parkandocean.com/full-moon-kayak-tours

SCREAM "GOOOOOAL!"
AT AN INTER MIAMI GAME

The newest team in South Florida is Inter Miami, owned by famed footballer David Beckham. DRV PNK Stadium fits more than 19,000 members of the team's growing fan base, and at the northern goal line you'll find super fans who call themselves La Familia, composed of Vice City 1896, the Siege, and Southern Legion. At each game, the groups bang on drums, lead chants and songs, wave flags and banners, and are always dressed in the team's black-and-pink regalia with a flamingo on the crest. During the game, fuel up with bites from the concession stands, paired well with a beer or two from the stadium concourse. Whether Inter Miami wins or loses, follow La Familia off the field for an impromptu dance party.

1350 NW 55th St., 305-428-0603
intermiamicf.com

HANG OUT WITH THOUSANDS OF BUTTERFLIES

AT BUTTERFLY WORLD

Just west of Fort Lauderdale is Coconut Creek, also known as the Butterfly Capital of the World. That's because nestled inside Tradewinds Park is Butterfly World, three acres of botanical gardens and aviaries filled with 20,000 butterflies, as well as several varieties of exotic birds. As part of his quest to study and raise butterflies, the park was founded by Ronald Boender in 1988, making it the first butterfly house in the United States. Butterfly World is a working butterfly farm, and three decades later, it is credited with helping save the Schaus Swallowtail. Guests are invited to step inside the butterfly aviaries, where they'll be surrounded by the fluttering insects; if you stay still, butterflies will certainly land atop your head, shoulders, or arms.

3600 W Sample Rd., Coconut Creek, 954-977-4434
butterflyworld.com

STRETCH AND SHOP
AT THE LOOP

If there were ever such a thing as an outdoor community center, it would be Las Olas Oceanside Park (LOOP). Here, Fort Lauderdale gathers for yoga, farmers markets, live music, annual beach cleanups, and a celebration of the city's parks. Each Saturday is an all-day farmers, antiques, and artisan market, where you can find everything from cheeses and fresh produce to jewelry and handmade wares. Every other week is Sundays by the Shore, an event with live music, restorative yoga, a marketplace, and lawn games. If fitness is your thing, check out the schedule for full moon yoga, sunrise workouts, cardio sessions, HIIT training, and Yoga on the Lawn. The LOOP consists of four green spaces in the city: Las Olas Oceanside Park, Las Olas Intracoastal Promenade Park, The Sunset Terrace at the Las Olas Beach Garage, and DC Alexander Park.

theloopflb.com

FIND NESTING LOGGERHEADS
ON A SEA TURTLE WALK

Sea turtle season runs from March 1 to October 31, and during the summertime hatchlings emerge from their nests to follow the moon toward the ocean. Nature lovers can safely explore the sea turtle nesting grounds on Fort Lauderdale Beach with guides from the Museum of Discovery and Science (MODS). Groups will meet at the museum for a presentation about the different types of sea turtles—the most common in the Sunshine State are loggerheads—and the importance of protecting the species. Then, guides will lead the groups onto the dark beaches in search of nesting turtles. Make sure you have your phone lights off to avoid disturbing the creatures. It's not guaranteed that you'll spot a sea turtle nest on every trip, but the experience and education make it worth the trip.

401 SW 2nd St., 954-467-6637
mods.org

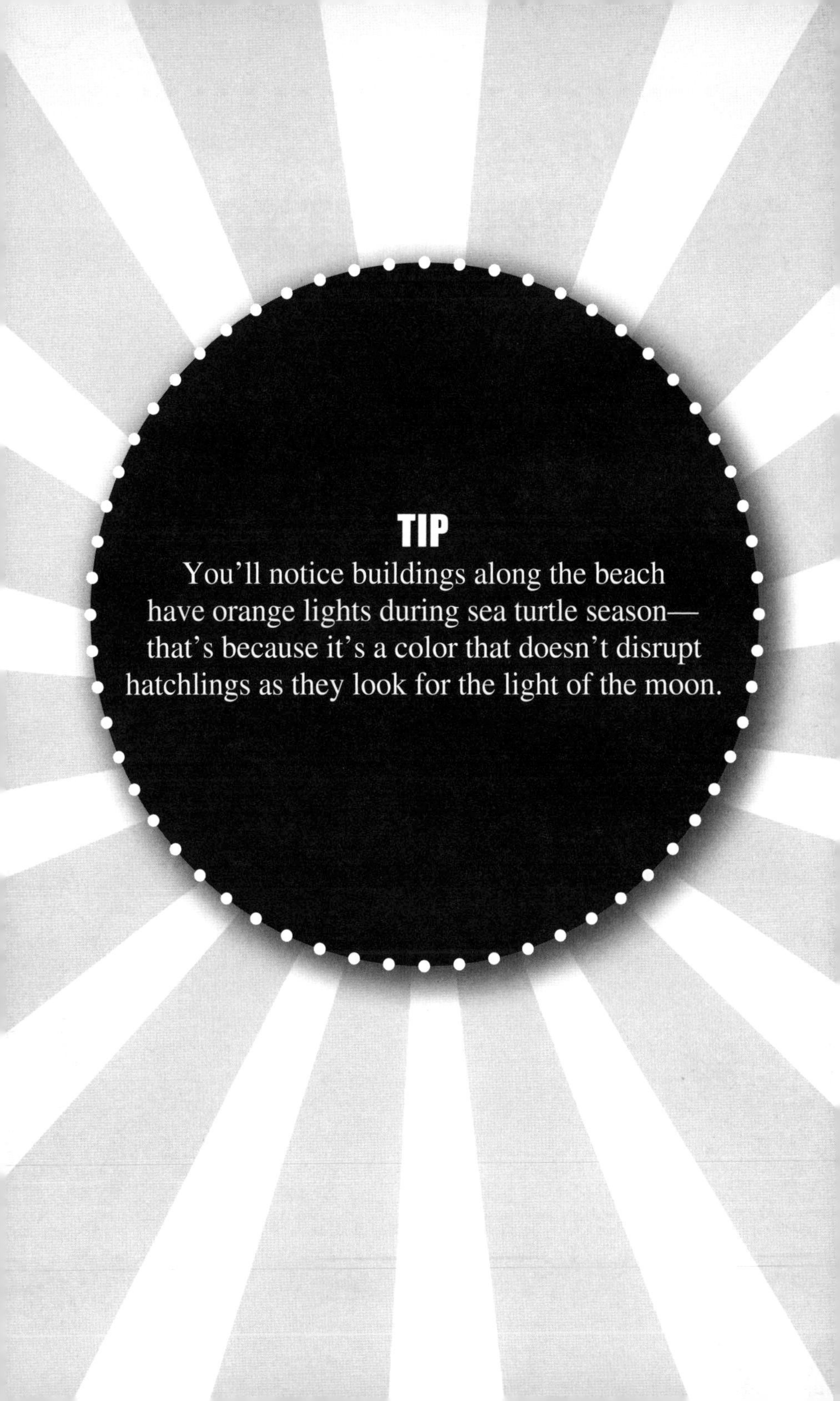

TIP

You'll notice buildings along the beach have orange lights during sea turtle season—that's because it's a color that doesn't disrupt hatchlings as they look for the light of the moon.

SING THE FIGHT SONG
DURING A MIAMI DOLPHINS FOOTBALL GAME

For Dolphins fans, 1972 was a year that will forever go down in history as the year that Coach Don Shula took the team to the Super Bowl after completing "the perfect season" with zero losses. The street where Hard Rock Stadium is located was named after Shula and for Floridians, his 2020 death was a tragedy, but each year fans hope the team will be one year closer to repeating the magic of 1972. Throw on your turquoise and orange, throw a "fins up" sign (the blade of your hand to the forehead), dance along with the cheerleading team, and sing the fight song—not the 2009 remix by Pitbull and T-Pain. If you're lucky enough to be in town for a home game against the New York Jets (a.k.a. sworn enemies of Dolphins fans), snag a ticket to see the teams battle it out on the field.

347 Don Shula Dr., Miami Gardens, 305-943-8000
miamidolphins.com

STRAP ON YOUR SCUBA TANK

AND EXPLORE SHIPWRECKS

Whether you're SCUBA certified or more comfortable with a snorkel and fins, the undersea world of Fort Lauderdale and its neighbors has plenty of shipwrecks to traverse. Advanced divers can visit the *Guy Harvey* in Fort Lauderdale, named for the marine artist who painted a mural along the *Lady Kimberly* freighter before sinking it. There's also Shipwreck Park in Pompano Beach, where the 1967 *Lady Luck* and 1970 *Okinawa* have been converted into public art pieces. The park raises money to create artificial reefs, expand the diving experience, and spread awareness about the importance of coral reefs. Open-water divers or snorkelers should check out the S.S. *Copenhagen* in Lauderdale-By-The-Sea, the *Ancient Mariner* and the Separated Rocks reef in Deerfield Beach, or the *Miss Dania Beach* in Hollywood.

Shipwreck Park
shipwreckparkpompano.org

South Florida Diving
southfloridadiving.com

57

THROW A RUBBER RAT ONTO THE RINK

AT A FLORIDA PANTHERS HOCKEY GAME

With so many northern transplants in the Fort Lauderdale area, it's no wonder that we've got a National Hockey League team of our very own. The Florida Panthers practice and play out of the FLA Live Arena in Sunrise, which is also used as a performance venue. A tradition that has become synonymous with the hockey team is a barrage of rats thrown onto the ice after a win—rubber rats, of course. The celebration supposedly dates back to the '90s when former Panther Scott Mellanby killed a rat in the locker room by swatting it against the wall with his hockey stick and then went on to score two goals. After that, fans began throwing rubber rats onto the rink after every goal as a ritual for good luck. In the interest of time (and the staff), fans now only throw the toys onto the rink at the end of a winning game.

1 Panther Pkwy., Sunrise, 954-835-7000
nhl.com/panthers

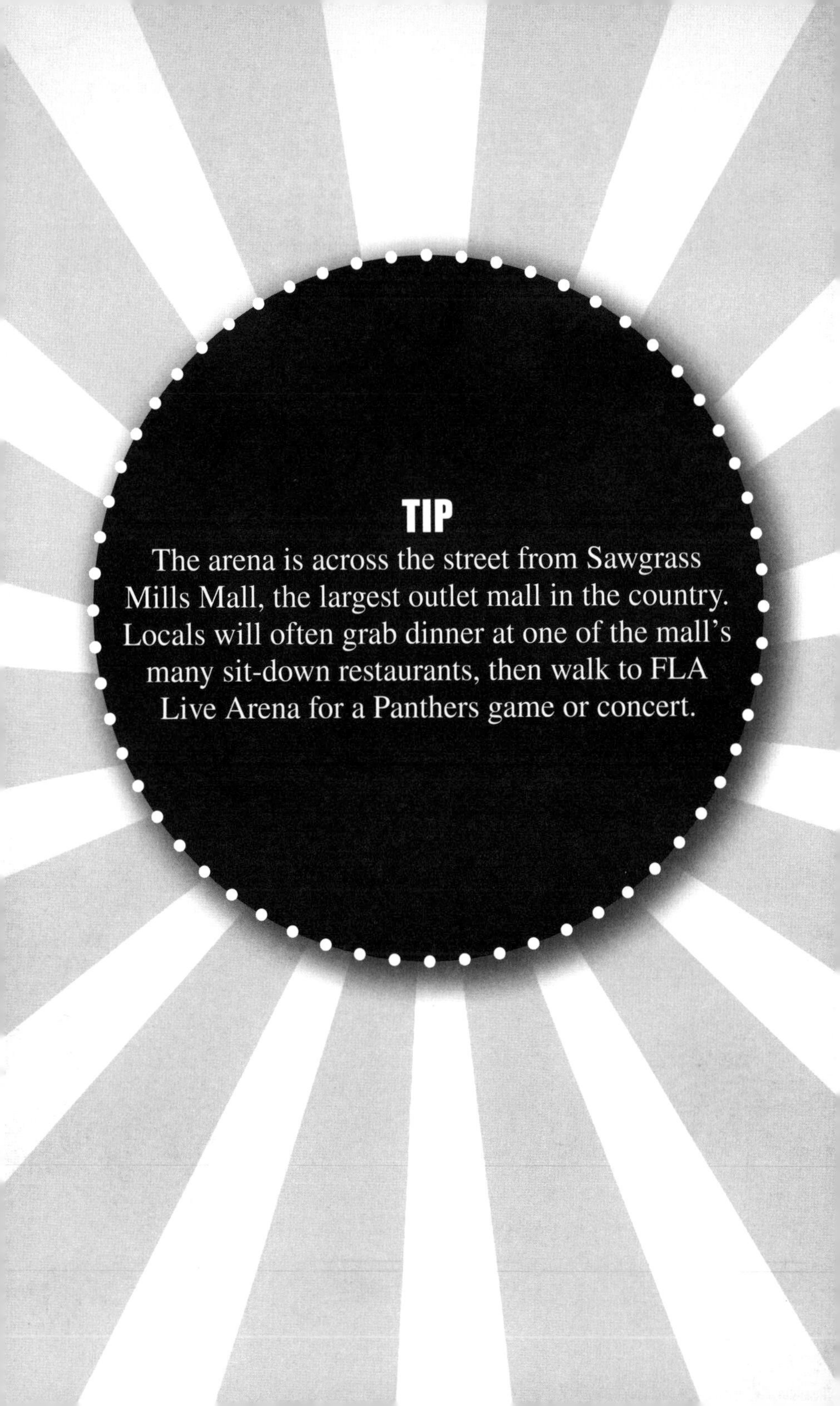

TIP

The arena is across the street from Sawgrass Mills Mall, the largest outlet mall in the country. Locals will often grab dinner at one of the mall's many sit-down restaurants, then walk to FLA Live Arena for a Panthers game or concert.

EXPERIENCE THE NEW RIVER AND BEYOND
BY WATER TAXI

Why walk when you can ride? For more than two decades, the Water Taxi has been one of the most relaxing ways to get around Fort Lauderdale. Traversing the New River and the Intracoastal Waterway, the Water Taxi has 10 stops throughout Fort Lauderdale with the southernmost stop located at Margaritaville in Hollywood. Riders can purchase an all-day or evening pass to hop on and off as they please; there are also sunset cruises on Fridays and Saturdays. For the Hollywood Express, climb aboard at Stop 4 in Fort Lauderdale to be dropped off at Jimmy Buffett's 5 O'Clock Somewhere Bar. There are different sized boats, too, with bars on the double-deckers and coolers of beer, wine, and canned cocktails on mid-sized vessels. Even if you have no place to go, ride the Water Taxi for the guided tour to learn about the mega mansions, Fort Lauderdale history, and to see impressive yachts up close.

watertaxi.com

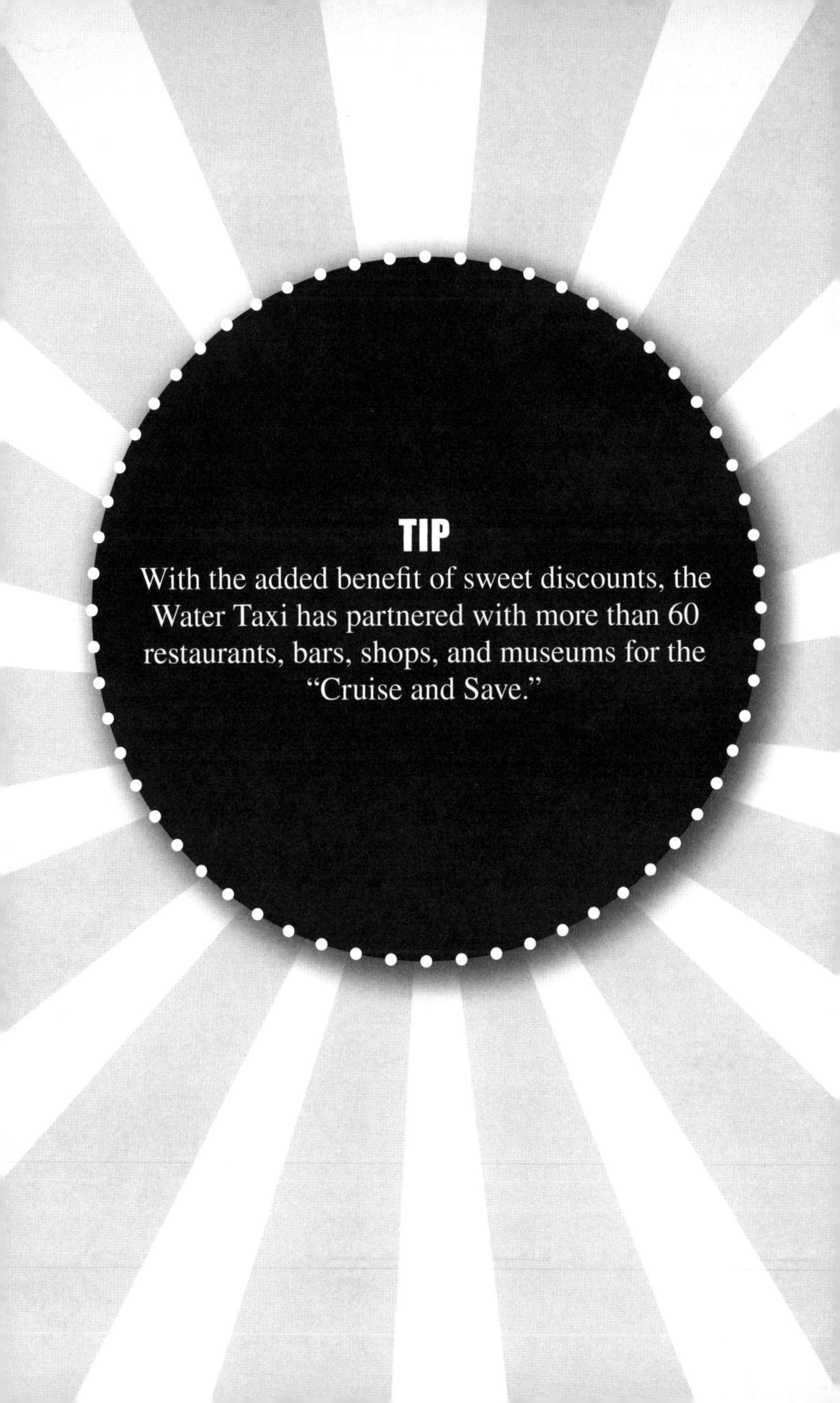

TIP

With the added benefit of sweet discounts, the Water Taxi has partnered with more than 60 restaurants, bars, shops, and museums for the "Cruise and Save."

BET ON THE PONIES
AT GULFSTREAM PARK

Thanks to Greater Fort Lauderdale's weather, horse racing takes place 10 months out of the year at Gulfstream Park in Hallandale Beach, south of Fort Lauderdale. The park hosts major tournaments like the Pegasus World Cup and Florida Derby. During these live race days, sit in the stands or view the races from the comfort of a dining table at Ten Palms, which overlooks the track measuring a little over one mile in circumference. New to horse racing? Racing ambassadors at Gulfstream's guest services booth are on hand to guide newbies through the basics of the sport and help with the self-service tote machines. Guests can also enjoy the races from the Carousel Club, an outdoor venue just steps away from the track. This is just one of countless restaurants, shops, and entertainment options at the park.

901 S Federal Hwy., Hallandale Beach, 954-454-7000
gulfstreampark.com

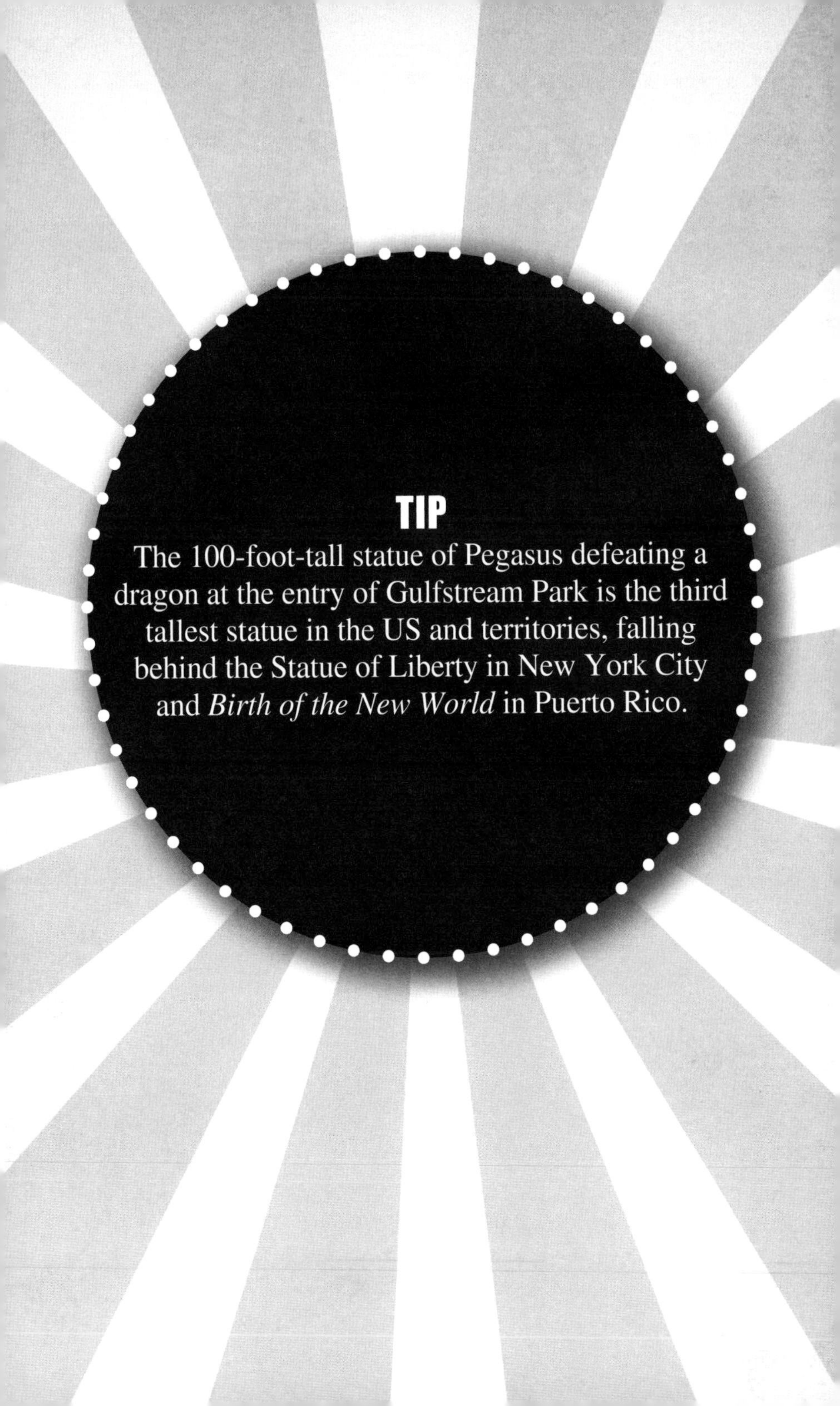

TIP

The 100-foot-tall statue of Pegasus defeating a dragon at the entry of Gulfstream Park is the third tallest statue in the US and territories, falling behind the Statue of Liberty in New York City and *Birth of the New World* in Puerto Rico.

COLLECT MINI LOBSTERS
DURING BUGFEST

A summertime tradition in the beach town of Lauderdale-By-The-Sea, BugFest is the kick off to mini lobster ("bug") season. For two days, bug hunters dive into the Atlantic Ocean off the shores of the town in search of these tasty crustaceans, and each diver is allowed to catch up to 12 mini lobsters per day (only six if you're in the Florida Keys). There are designated weigh stations around town, and there are thousands of dollars in cash and dive gear prizes given away for the largest lobsters caught by divers in different categories. A launch party is hosted each year, as well as seminars, culinary contests, and parties to celebrate the year's catch.

discoverlbts.com/bugfest

RIDE AN AIRBOAT
THROUGH THE EVERGLADES

When author Marjory Stoneman Douglas first saw the Everglades, she called it "the river of grass"—and from atop an airboat, you can see why. At Everglades Holiday Park, take an hour-long ride with the whole family in search of the glassy eyes of an American alligator, white feathers of an ibis, and water droplets rolling off a giant water lily pad. Other activities at the park include a trip to Gator Boys, a rescue park featuring gator wrestling and the chance to hold a baby alligator. Finally, the private, 45-minute Animal Encounter allows visitors to interact with five different animals, take photos, and learn about the mammals and reptiles that reside in the Everglades.

21940 Griffin Rd., 954-434-8111
evergladesholidaypark.com

TIP

Even if you're not an early riser, taking a morning airboat ride through the Everglades is a breath-taking experience.

62

CHECK OUT MEGA MANSIONS FROM THE *JUNGLE QUEEN*

Fort Lauderdale's nickname is the Venice of America, thanks to its 165 miles of waterways through the city. While there are endless yachts and fishing boats that make their way through canals, rivers, and the Intracoastal, the vessel that has reigned supreme since the city's early days is the *Jungle Queen* riverboat. A source of both entertainment and education, guests hop aboard the boat to see the luxe mansions on Millionaire's Row, learn the history of Fort Lauderdale, and enjoy dinner and a Polynesian-themed show. The original riverboat was built in Jacksonville and brought down to Fort Lauderdale by Captain Al in 1935, launching a beloved tradition. Today, the company offers two cruises—a 90-minute sightseeing cruise twice daily and an Island Dinner & Show cruise in the evening.

801 Seabreeze Blvd., 954-462-5596
junglequeen.com

HIKE THROUGH
HUGH TAYLOR BIRCH STATE PARK

Situated between the Intracoastal Waterway and the beach, you'd never guess you're in the middle of urban Fort Lauderdale when you stand beneath the canopy of oak trees at Hugh Taylor Birch State Park. The 140-acre park was gifted by the park's namesake, who also purchased the adjacent Bonnet House for his daughter as a wedding present. Hikes through the park are low impact and enjoyable, being that Florida is notoriously flat (the highest point in South Florida is less than 100 feet above sea level). If the gopher tortoises can do it, so can you! Other activities in the park include kayaking, bicycling, fishing, camping, and paddleboarding. Leashed dogs are welcome, too!

3109 E Sunrise Blvd., 954-564-4521
floridastateparks.org/hughtaylorbirch

TIP

After a jaunt through the park, reward yourself by stopping at Park & Ocean, the park's indoor-outdoor dining venue, for a beer and light bites beneath sea grape trees.

WAVE A RAINBOW FLAG
AT PRIDE

Fort Lauderdale and its neighboring cities have a large LGBTQ population, so Pride is no small affair, serving as a tourist destination for the vibrant community. Wilton Manors, nicknamed "the gayborhood," hosts Stonewall Pride each June with a two-day party, consisting of a street festival and parade. There's even a Pride flag-raising ceremony at city hall to launch Pride festivities! Pride Month is typically celebrated in June, coinciding with the anniversary of the Stonewall Riots in New York City that kick-started the equality movement. But summer months are brutal in South Florida, so Pride Fort Lauderdale is hosted in November on the beach, complete with the parade and various parties—and that just means more Pride for everyone!

Pride Fort Lauderdale
pridefortlauderdale.org

Stonewall Pride Wilton Manors
stonewallpride.lgbt

EAT AND DRINK ON A FLOATING TIKI BAR

WITH CRUISIN' TIKIS

Whether it's a birthday or bachelorette party, or just because it's the weekend, there's no need to leave the bar behind when you want to hit the water. With Cruisin' Tikis, a literal floating tiki bar, you and five friends can hop aboard the boat with a licensed captain for a unique day of floating down the New River. Book this fun cruise with optional waterfront stops, the sandbar trip to anchor on the Intracoastal and swim, a sunset cruise, or a late-night jazz cruise. Cruisin' Tikis meets guests at the Historic Downtowner and will provide the ice and cooler; it's up to you to bring your favorite drinks and snacks to enjoy on the water.

10 S New River Dr. E, 833-386-8454
cruisintikisfortlauderdale.com

TIP

After meeting at the Historic Downtowner, Tiki-goers can opt to take a meal to go for the trip or get lunch from the iconic tavern before or after the jaunt on the water.

BE A SEA CAPTAIN FOR A DAY

AT THE FORT LAUDERDALE INTERNATIONAL BOAT SHOW

Not surprisingly, Fort Lauderdale is considered the yachting capital of the world (Says who? We don't know, but we'll take the title). So it only makes sense that each fall the city plays host to the Fort Lauderdale International Boat Show, a five-day celebration of all things boating. That includes the Superyacht Village at the Pier Sixty-Six Hotel & Marina, countless seminars, demonstrations at the AquaZone, contests, plenty of food, and exhibitions of the latest in yachting and fishing. And being on the water, sustainability is key at FLIBS, which has initiatives such as using 100% renewable energy during the show.

Fort Lauderdale International Boat Show
(at Bahia Mar Fort Lauderdale Beach)
801 Seabreeze Blvd.
flibs.com

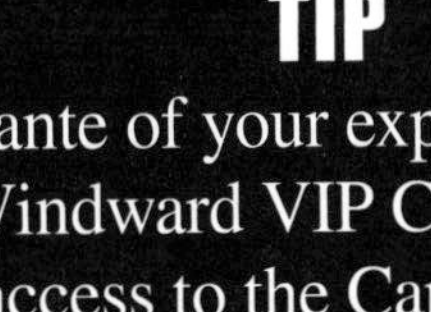

TIP

To up the ante of your experience at FLIBS, opt for the Windward VIP Club experience. This gives guests access to the Captain's Lounge with a premium open bar, private concierge, Water Taxi service, and impeccable views of the water.

CAST A LINE AND CATCH DINNER
FROM A PIER

Ocean breeze, salt air, and sun on your face—how else would you rather catch your dinner? Both experienced and novice fishermen can enjoy a day of fishing at the many beautiful piers in Greater Fort Lauderdale. Different piers offer different accommodations, such as renting fishing poles, but all have bait and tackle shops from which to purchase accessories as well as drinks and snacks. Expect to find fish like snapper, mackerel, pompano, or snook at the end of your line, and be sure to keep it away from the curious pelicans that make their way to the piers. If fishing isn't in the cards for you, the pier is still a destination worth adding to your list as a sightseer to see the fishing in action or to just enjoy a quiet place to watch the waves roll in.

TIP

From a bird's eye view, the end of the pier in Pompano Beach is in the shape of a pompano fish, fit with a peephole "eye" that you can fish out of.

International Fishing Pier
200 NE 21st Ave., Deerfield Beach, 954-480-4407

Fisher Family Pier
222 N Pompano Beach Blvd., Pompano Beach
954-482-3229

Dania Beach Fishing Pier
100 N Beach Rd., Dania Beach, 954-924-6800

A display at Ah-Tah-Thi-Ki Museum, the official museum of the Seminole tribe.

CULTURE AND HISTORY

STEP BACK IN TIME
WITH HISTORY FORT LAUDERDALE

While South Florida may not be anywhere close to old compared to other communities in the country, we're proud of our unique heritage. Formerly the New River Inn, the History Fort Lauderdale building was erected in 1905 to house guests in the burgeoning riverfront town. Visitors to the museum are invited to explore the first floor for free and the second with admission, and all the displays can be translated into French, Spanish, or Brazilian Portuguese simply by scanning a QR code. For the full experience, opt for the walking tour with a knowledgeable guide. Not only will you get to see the museum, but also the 1907 King-Cromartie House, which is the first home of Ivy Stranahan née Cromartie, who was the city's first teacher at the 1899 schoolhouse. The schoolhouse is also a stop on the tour.

219 SW 2nd Ave., 954-463-4431
historyfortlauderdale.org

TIP

Love a good ghost story? Join History Fort Lauderdale for its monthly ghost tour of the historical district. You won't just stand before haunted buildings; guides will take you inside to tell stories about the paranormal activity reported over the years and even listen to recordings of electronic voice phenomena (EVP), or alleged "spirit voices" picked up by electronic devices. Spooky!

MEET FORT LAUDERDALE'S FOUNDERS

AT THE HISTORIC STRANAHAN HOUSE

A two-story bungalow on the New River, the Stranahan House was home to Frank and Ivy Stranahan, considered the founders of Fort Lauderdale. Ivy became the area's first schoolteacher in 1899, educating the nine children of other founding families in a small schoolhouse. Frank made his way to Fort Lauderdale for the same reason many other men did at the time, for the job opportunities to work on the river alongside the Seminole locals. After marrying in 1900, the couple built their home on the banks of the New River in 1901, which also housed the trading post and post office. A tiny structure for mail is still on the property! The Stranahan House served as a residence until Ivy's death in 1971, and today visitors can take part in multiple guided tours each day. The venue has also served as a place where many a set of lovebirds have tied the knot.

335 SE 6th Ave., 954-524-4736
stranahanhouse.org

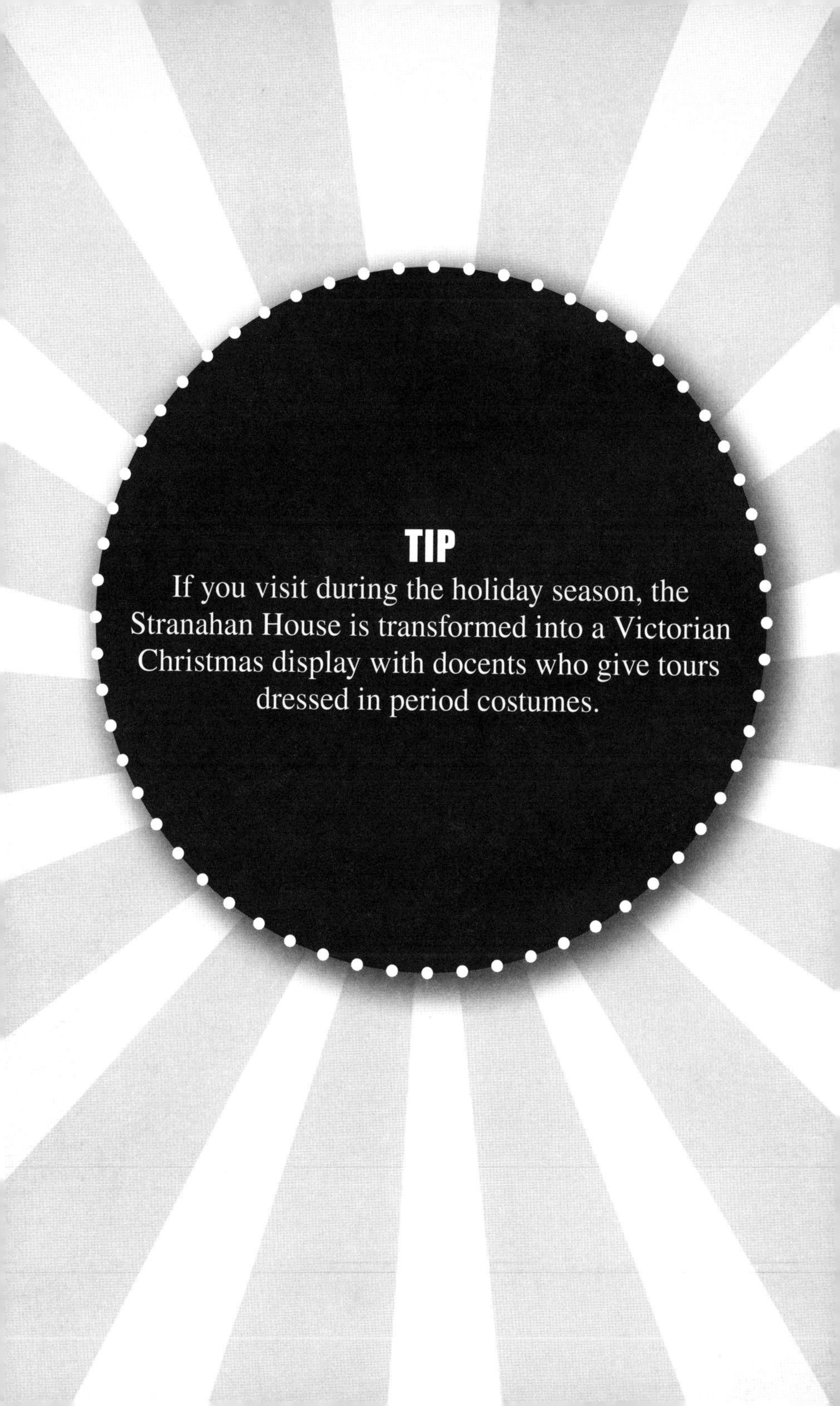
TIP
If you visit during the holiday season, the Stranahan House is transformed into a Victorian Christmas display with docents who give tours dressed in period costumes.

SEE THE GAVEL THAT OVERTURNED "DON'T ASK, DON'T TELL" AT THE STONEWALL NATIONAL MUSEUM & ARCHIVES

LGBTQ history and culture comes alive at Fort Lauderdale's Stonewall National Museum & Archives, considered one of the largest gay archives and libraries in the United States. The nonprofit museum, founded in 1972, is named for the Stonewall Riots of 1969 in New York City, considered the kick-off to the equality movement for the LGBTQ community. The museum covers a wealth of topics that have touched the community, such as HIV/AIDS, marriage equality, the lavender scare, and pop culture, but they have an impressive collection of posters, photographs, buttons, artwork, books, and items such as the gavel Nancy Pelosi used to overturn "Don't Ask, Don't Tell." Check the museum's website before visiting, because Stonewall also plays host to author presentations, panels, exhibits, film screenings, and special events all year long.

1300 E Sunrise Blvd., 954-763-8565
stonewall-museum.org

PEEK THROUGH THE MEGALODON MOUTH

AT THE MUSEUM OF DISCOVERY AND SCIENCE

The wonders of science begin before even setting foot inside the Museum of Discovery and Science (MODS), as visitors young and old will be enamored with the 52-foot-tall gravity clock that tells time with the clanking of balls running through a series of rails. Other permanent attractions include the friendly otters playing in their two-story home, a giant Megalodon mouth, learning labs, the outdoor Science Park, and a chance to watch an incoming (simulated!) hurricane at the storm center. Throughout the year, visiting exhibitions are included with interactive elements to teach scientists young and old about the human body, environment, health, engineering, and more. Also on the campus is the IMAX theater, for science-themed 3D films as well as new releases to be experienced in a big way.

401 SW 2nd St., 954-467-6637
mods.org

EMBRACE ART BY A QUIRKY COUPLE

AT THE BONNET HOUSE MUSEUM & GARDENS

A wedding gift from Hugh Taylor Birch (a nearby park is named after him) to his daughter Helen and her artist husband Frederic Clay Bartlett, the Bonnet House was a southern retreat from Chicago's blustery winters. After Helen's death, Bartlett remarried Evelyn Fortune Lilly, a self-taught painter, and the two turned the Caribbean plantation-style property into a living ode to art and nature, from the orchid house and decorative ceilings to seashells embedded into the walls and rooms overflowing with paintings. Throughout the home, guests can spot places where Bartlett painted furniture and walls to look like marble and natural stone. Evelyn lived in the home until 1995 and died two years later at the age of 109. The manse is now under the care of the Florida Trust for Historic Preservation and is enjoyed by locals and visitors to Fort Lauderdale alike—a quirky abode envisioned by two creative spirits.

900 N Birch Rd., 954-563-5393
bonnethouse.org

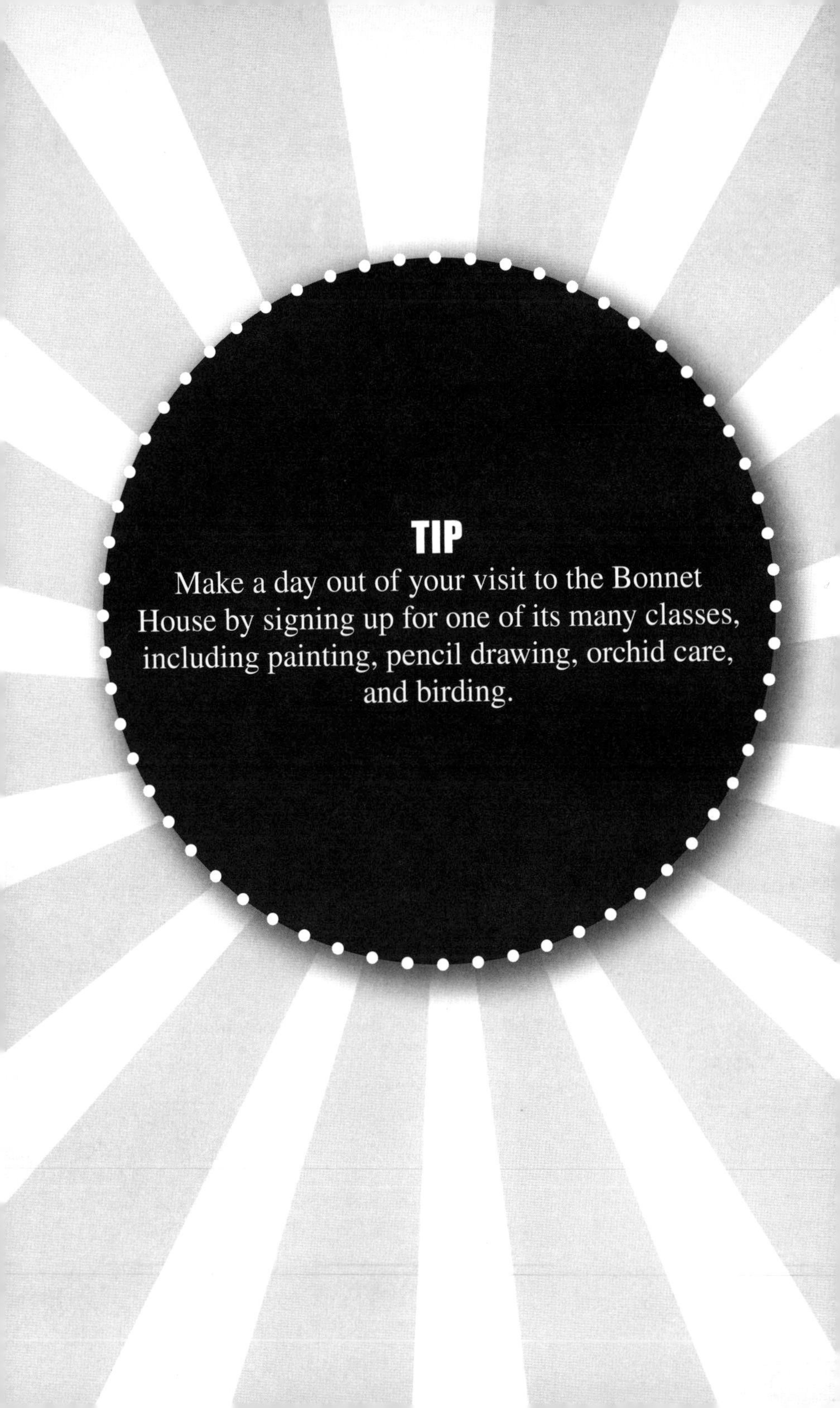
TIP
Make a day out of your visit to the Bonnet House by signing up for one of its many classes, including painting, pencil drawing, orchid care, and birding.

73

CELEBRATE SEMINOLE CULTURE AT AH-TAH-THI-KI

Located on the Big Cypress Reservation, the journey to Ah-Tah-Thi-Ki will have you driving through the swamps down winding Snake Road and passing the Ahfachkee School and rodeo grounds—just part of the experience and privilege of visiting the Seminole tribe. The campus serves as "a place to learn, a place to remember," as indicated by its name in Miccosukee, with not just a museum but also a laboratory for conserving artifacts and a library for scholars and researchers. Ah-Tah-Thi-Ki has the largest collection of Southeastern beadwork outside of the Smithsonian National Museum of the American Indian in Washington, DC, as well as historical documents and a vault filled with precious oral history. The museum also works to promote the culture by hosting contemporary art exhibits; showcasing modern beadwork, basket weaving, and patchwork; and celebrating southeastern tribal communities.

34725 W Boundary Rd., Clewiston, (Big Cypress Seminole Indian Reservation), 877-902-1113
ahtahthiki.com

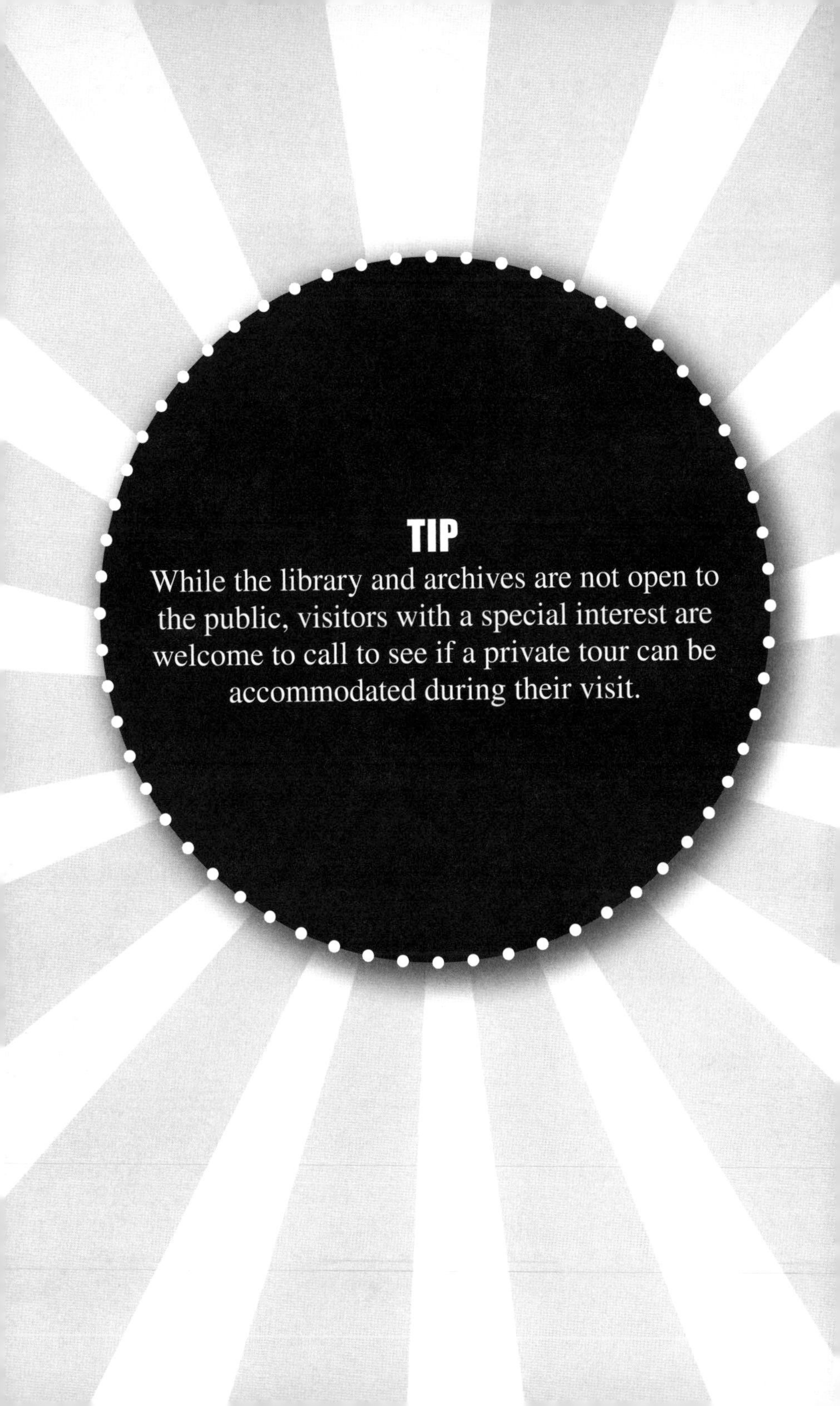
TIP
While the library and archives are not open to the public, visitors with a special interest are welcome to call to see if a private tour can be accommodated during their visit.

SEE THE COLORS DRIP DOWN

THE NSU MUSEUM OF ART FORT LAUDERDALE

You can't miss the art museum in downtown Fort Lauderdale, thanks to the *Acid-Free* mural by Jen Stark of a neon rainbow dripping down the side. The piece is one of three outdoor murals and the art continues inside with permanent and rotating exhibitions throughout its 25,000 square feet of exhibition space, along with thousands of pieces that have been digitized for its online collection. Known for its emphasis on Latin American and contemporary art, NSU Museum of Art Fort Lauderdale pays special attention to women, Black and Latino/a artists, and African art. On the first Thursday of the month, the museum hosts Sunny Days and Starry Nights with free admission and two-for-one glasses of wine from the Museum Café all day. Be sure to check the calendar for lectures, film screenings, and one-on-one conversations with artists of all disciplines held in the museum's auditorium.

1 E Las Olas Blvd., 954-525-5500
nsuartmuseum.org

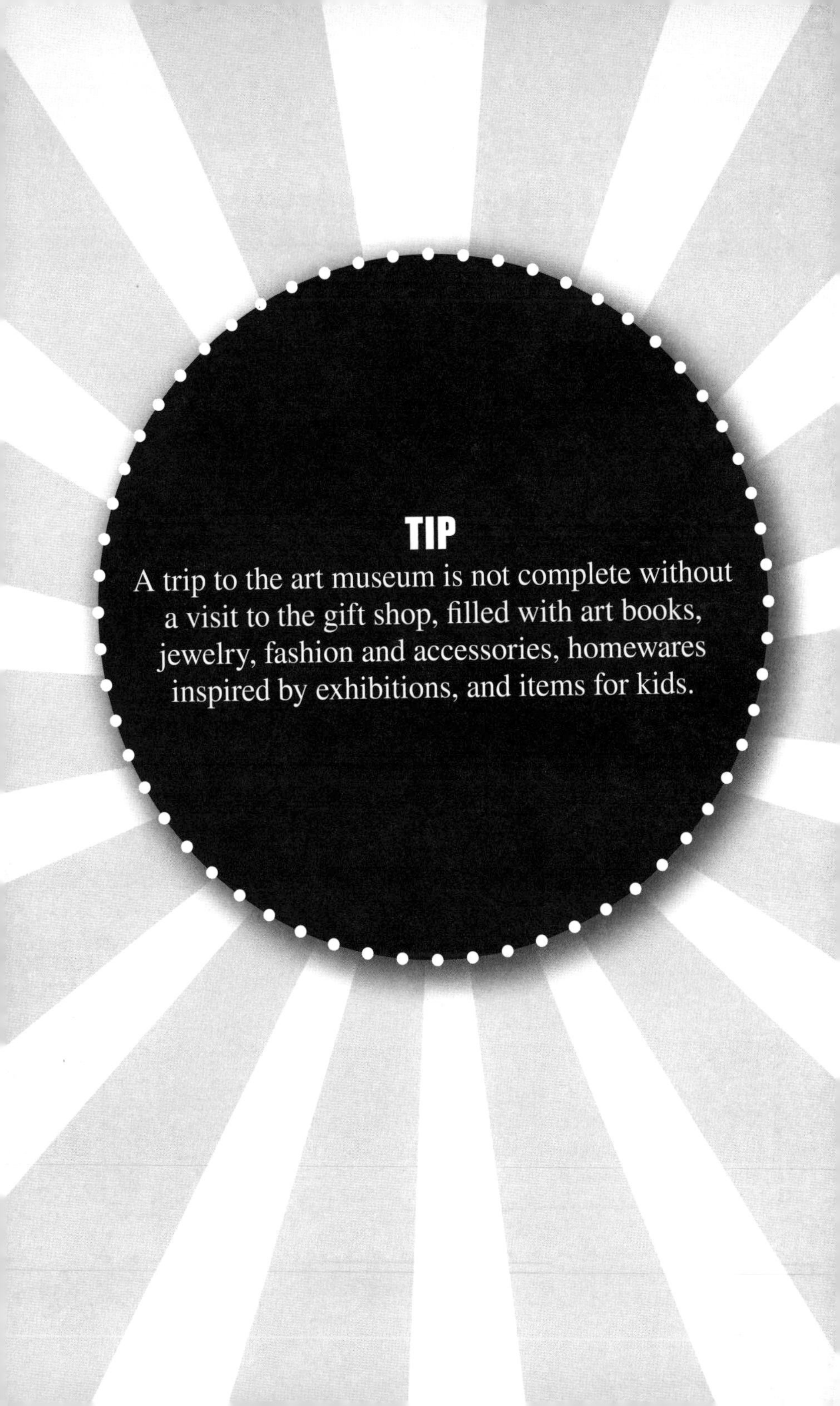
TIP
A trip to the art museum is not complete without a visit to the gift shop, filled with art books, jewelry, fashion and accessories, homewares inspired by exhibitions, and items for kids.

ENJOY THE VIEW
FROM THE RIVERSIDE HOTEL

There are plenty of hotels and highrises scattered throughout downtown Fort Lauderdale, but the lime green building with international flags flying from the second floor has made its mark since 1936. Originally named the Champ Carr Hotel, the Riverside Hotel was founded by Chicago brothers Preston and John Wells at a time when finer accommodations were in demand for blossoming Fort Lauderdale. Today, guests can lodge in the original hotel tower or opt for a room in the executive tower from floors nine through twelve for stunning views of Las Olas Boulevard's twinkling lights and beyond. Dining options abound at the Riverside Hotel: Wild Sea Las Olas and the Golden Lyon Vintage Pub on the Las Olas Boulevard-facing side of the hotel, Preston's Wine & Martini Lounge inside, and Boathouse on the Riverfront.

620 E Las Olas Blvd., 954-467-0671
riversidehotel.com

TIP

Want more experiences from up above? Check out rooftop bars in downtown Fort Lauderdale like Rooftop @1WLO, The Easton, and Sparrow at The Dalmar.

RELIVE THE PIONEER DAYS
AT THE OLD DAVIE SCHOOL HISTORICAL MUSEUM

As settlers began to move into the Everglades and make it more habitable for families, there was a need for a schoolhouse. When the town outgrew the makeshift classrooms, the Davie School was designed by August Geiger and opened its doors to a class of 90 students in 1918. The two-story school served multiple purposes for the town, including a town hall, dance hall, school board office, and shelter during floods and hurricanes. The Davie School was in use until 1980, but its memory is kept alive as a living schoolhouse for visitors to take a step back into the 1920s. On the campus of the museum are the Viele and Walsh-Osterhoudt homes, a recreated 1909 pioneer home, and a recreated citrus packing house. Inside, visitors can see photographs, maps, ephemera, and artifacts from yesteryear. Throughout the year, the museum schedules special events for the holidays, as well as ghost tours, crafting classes, and walking tours.

6650 Griffin Rd., Davie, 954-797-1044
olddavieschool.org

77

SEE OLYMPIC MEDALS
AT THE INTERNATIONAL SWIMMING HALL OF FAME

Long before Fort Lauderdale was the Spring Break capital of the nation (dare we say world?), it was the premier spring training ground for collegiate swimmers. Each winter, teams made their way south for practice and would return home to tell their fellow students about the party scene, kickstarting Spring Break mania. At the International Swimming Hall of Fame, the museum pays tribute to the aquatic sports and their impact on all walks of life, from film and fashion to history and civil rights. Memorabilia include props from the *Tarzan* movies starring Johnny Weissmuller (who lived in Fort Lauderdale), Olympic flags and medals, underwater photos of the *Titanic*, a sculptural relief of Assyrian swimmers, and more. After a $137 million renovation, the building includes new swimming pools, a 27-meter dive tower, amenity deck, grandstand, restaurant, and updated museum space.

1 Hall of Fame Dr., 954-462-6536
ishof.org

HAND FEED THE PEACOCKS
AT FLAMINGO GARDENS

Once the 1927 home of Floyd L. and Jane Wray, Flamingo Gardens is now a botanical garden and wildlife sanctuary filled with exotic fruit trees, rosy flamingos, and eye-catching peacocks who prowl the grounds and fly into the orchid-tangled branches of the oaks and banyan trees. The property includes some of the original buildings from the Wrays, as well as more than 3,000 species of plants and trees, more than 90 native species, and the largest tree in Florida: a 102-foot-tall Cluster Fig. Guided trolley rides are offered throughout the day, allowing guests to see more of the gardens and sanctuary. If you and the family get hungry, make a stop at the Flamingo Cafe or Garden Grill for some grub.

3750 S Flamingo Rd., Davie, 954-473-2955
flamingogardens.org

TIP

Buying bird food to feed the peacocks at the gift shop is worth it—they aren't shy and will nibble straight from your hand.

FIND YOUR NEW FAVORITE ARTIST
AT THE LAS OLAS ART FAIR

Why host an art fair once a year when you can do it three times, instead? That's the sentiment behind the Las Olas Art Fair, the biggest juried art festival in Fort Lauderdale. The outdoor affair brings together artists from around the country over three weekends every year, in the cooler months of January, March and October. Over these weekends, tree-lined Las Olas Boulevard is closed off to vehicles to make it a pedestrian-friendly, free event for collectors and the curious. Along the boulevard, artists stand with their artwork ready to answer questions, make a sale, or garner connections for future commissions. Pieces vary in price, from handmade wearable art for a few dollars to high-end paintings in the tens of thousands.

artfestival.com

TIP

Continue the art experience by visiting Las Olas Boulevard's art galleries, like the New River Fine Art Gallery, Sienna Fine Art, and Bellagio International Gallery.

SAIL TO SCALE

THE HILLSBORO POINT LIGHTHOUSE

Driving down A1A at night, drivers are treated to a vintage light show while passing by the fully automated Hillsboro Point Lighthouse. While the technology is much different than it was back in 1906, it's still a majestic sight to see at night, with the lens spinning and illuminating the beach. The lighthouse was made in Detroit in 1906 and its Fresnel lens came all the way from Paris. It has guided ships to shore from Hillsboro Point in Florida since 1907 and its light has never wavered, thanks to countless keepers over the years. Lighthouse staff host tours only once a month, with multiple shuttle sails from Pompano Beach to the lighthouse.

2700 N Ocean Blvd., Pompano Beach, 954-942-2102
hillsborolighthouse.org/museum

BE MOVED
AT THE WORLD AIDS MUSEUM

The humble World AIDS Museum's mission is to eliminate the stigma surrounding HIV/AIDS while preserving the history of its impact on humanity. Open since 2014 and the first of its kind, the main exhibit showcases the chronology of HIV/AIDS from the very first case to present day, including its impact on pop culture. Ancillary exhibits are a collection of art, multimedia, artifacts, and the Virtual Tapestry of Stories, a digital take on the AIDS quilt. The museum, located inside ArtServe, also hosts lectures, film screenings, poetry and book readings, art shows, and support groups. The ongoing Oral History Project strives to collect testimonials from people living with HIV/AIDS to give strength to their voices.

1350 E Sunrise Blvd., 954-390-0550
worldaidsmuseum.org

GO BACK TO SCHOOL
AT THE OLD DILLARD MUSEUM

In Fort Lauderdale's early days, Black children were segregated from their peers and attended Dillard School, the first public school for Black students. Prior to the school's opening in 1924, classes were held in private rooms, then moved into the one-room Colored School No. 11, built in 1907. Later, the Dillard School was built on land purchased from the city's founders, Frank and Ivy Stranahan. It was named in honor of James H. Dillard, who promoted education for Black children. As the city grew, more schools were built but the original has kept its place in the city's history. Today, it's listed on the National Register of Historic Places and is now a museum with exhibitions, art displays, and artifacts that celebrate the Black community in Fort Lauderdale.

1009 NW 4th St., 754-322-8828
browardschools.com/page/35769

83

SIT IN THE GIANT ADIRONDACK CHAIR
ON THE RIVERWALK

A walk along the riverfront is a quick way to see the many institutions that make Fort Lauderdale special, including the Broward Center, the Museum of Discovery and Science, endless restaurants, the Water Taxi cruising down the river, and the Stranahan House, the oldest surviving structure in the city. Whether you're out for a jog, walking your furry friend, or just strolling along Riverwalk, take a moment to jump up onto the oversized Adirondack chair with "Fort Lauderdale" painted along the top for a photo memory of your visit here. There are other Easter eggs along the route, including the Lone Sailor statue and a 9/11 memorial that was dedicated in 2020. The memorial, which includes a piece of the New York City PATH rail tracks destroyed in the terrorist attacks, overlooks the river and provides a quiet place to reflect and remember.

goriverwalk.com

GET YOUR SUGAR SKULL FIX
AT THE DAY OF THE DEAD

Sure, dressing up for Halloween is fun, but why stop there? The festivities continue in Fort Lauderdale with the annual Day of the Dead Festival. A part of Mexican tradition, *Dia de los Muertos* is a happy celebration to remember our loved ones who have passed on. The event begins with a candlelight vigil on November 2. The second event is a procession and parade of oversized skeleton puppets (the founder of the event is a celebrated puppeteer!) processional to the festival grounds. There, you'll find crafters, food stalls, live music, art exhibitions, and maybe even a *luchador* wrestler or two! In preparation for the big day, you'll want to turn yourself into a sugar skull by painting your face and adorning your hair with bright flowers. Leading up to the festivities is a whole schedule of happenings, including creating *ofrendas*, or altars in honor of the dead.

dayofthedeadflorida.com

SEE CHIHULY'S WORK UP CLOSE

AT THE WIENER MUSEUM OF DECORATIVE ARTS

A newer cultural institution in Greater Fort Lauderdale, the Wiener Museum of Decorative Arts (WMODA) opened its doors in 2014 as a celebration of glass and ceramic artwork. The Wiener family's collection includes pieces from the Art Deco, Art Nouveau, and Arts and Crafts eras, and big names from the classic blue-and-white porcelain stylings of Josiah Wedgwood to the lifelike creations of Sir Henry Doulton. Visitors to the museum can experience art from around the world including the French luxury crystal house Lalique, lauded Murano glass, and contemporary works by the Ardmore studio in South Africa. Of course, no collection would be complete without "hot glass" pieces by Dale Chihuly. The nonprofit museum boasts eight series by the glass artist as well as a few of his lesser-known acrylic works on paper.

481 S Federal Hwy., 2nd floor, Dania Beach, 954-376-6690
wmoda.com

REMEMBER THE WADE-IN OF 1961

ON FORT LAUDERDALE BEACH

Today, Fort Lauderdale Beach is a sunny paradise where people from all walks of life can enjoy a day on the sand—but it wasn't always that way. On the beach at the intersection of Las Olas Boulevard is a plaque commemorating the historic wade-ins during the summer of 1961, protests against the segregation of Fort Lauderdale's beaches. Starting on the Fourth of July, activists Eula Johnson and Dr. Von D. Mizell lead Black residents to take to the beach and enjoy a dip in the Atlantic Ocean; some protests had as many as 200 swimmers. The city struck back, bringing lawsuits against the two and the NAACP, which ultimately failed and led to the desegregation of the city's beaches. Their legacy is marked with the plaque, as well as renaming a park after the two heroes: the Dr. Von D. Mizell-Eula Johnson State Park in Hollywood.

fortlauderdale.gov

The Colonnade at Sawgrass Mills
Photo courtesy of Anthony J Rayburn, anthonyjrayburn.com

SHOPPING AND FASHION

PICK UP VINYL
AT RADIOACTIVE RECORDS

Vinyl disc records are making a comeback—or did they never go out of style? No matter your taste in music, this musical staple in Fort Lauderdale has a collection of vinyl from classical, country, and smooth jazz to hip-hop, punk, and comedy records, both old school and new releases. Customers can also find CDs, tapes, 8-tracks, gear for your turntable, and some tees for the memories. The owners host in-store listening parties and team up with local businesses for DJ sessions, movie events, and of course, National Record Store Day festivities every April.

845 N Federal Hwy., 954-762-9488
radio-active-records.com

TIP

The record store is just a few doors north of Roxanne's, a fun bar with a menu of cleverly named cocktails like Le Karen.

SHOP 'TIL YOU DROP
AT SAWGRASS MILLS MALL

At Sawgrass, shopping is a sport. The outlet mall boasts more than two million square feet of retail space, making it the largest outlet shopping center in the country. Its more than 350 stores include a range from street to high fashion, including Banana Republic, H&M, Neiman Marcus Last Call, Nordstrom Rack, Levi's, Michael Kors, and more. Luxury lovers should head straight to The Colonnade Outlets, a collection of more than 70 couture shops like Gucci, Balenciaga, Versace, Jimmy Choo, Fendi, and Tory Burch. If you work up an appetite from all the shopping, there are plenty of restaurants in which to refuel: Seasons 52, Grand Lux Cafe, Villagio, Zinburger, and Matchbox, to name a few.

12801 W Sunrise Blvd., Sunrise, 954-846-2350
simon.com/mall/sawgrass-mills

TIP

With a large out-of-town and international customer base, Sawgrass Mills has special services like currency exchange, valet parking, stroller rentals, and even a post office on site.

SEARCH FOR VINTAGE TREASURES

AT ODDBALLS NIFTY THRIFT

If vintage oddities light a fire in your soul, you'll feel right at home at OddBalls Nifty Thrift. And other shoppers agree: Yelp named the thrift store the third best in the country, rubbing elbows with stores in Chicago, Los Angeles, and Denver. Here, you'll find an endless cavern of rooms filled with furniture, clothing, books, magazines, comic books, typewriters, cameras, homewares, and niche memorabilia. Before you start shopping, though, stop by the store's bar to pick up a brew to enjoy as you try not to get lost in the thrift store itself. Don't forget to peek in the garden outside for road signs, plants, garden sculptures, and outdoor furniture.

4281 N Dixie Hwy., Oakland Park, 754-422-7623
facebook.com/oddballsniftythrift

TIP

Psst, the friendly owners are willing to bargain on items (within reason, of course).

90

CHANNEL YOUR INNER BEACH BABE

AT BRINY BOUTIQUE

When owner Alexa Chaviano opened her own clothing boutique, she called it "briny" as a nod to the salt air and ocean permeating through Fort Lauderdale. At Briny Boutique, she curates an affordable but high quality collection of quintessentially Florida pieces, from flowing maxi dresses and skirts to two-piece matching sets, rompers, and of course, cheeky swimwear. There are plenty of solid-colored pieces for minimalists and a healthy mix of bold prints for fashionistas who like to stand out in the crowd. Chaviano has shipments come in twice a week, too, so customers know they have the freshest looks when they step into her storefront.

470 N Federal Hwy., 954-552-0217
brinyboutique.com

TIP

Briny Boutique is conveniently located next to Doc B's, Foxy Brown, and Temple Street Eatery; perfect for an afternoon of shopping and lunch.

MAKE A DAY
OUT OF A TRIP TO DANIA POINTE

Visible from I-95 is the booming outdoor mall, Dania Pointe, a playground of shopping, dining, and activities for visitors of all ages. Here, fashion fiends will find their favorite stores like American Eagle, Anthropologie, Kendra Scott, Pandora, Sugarboo & Co., Tommy Bahama, and Urban Outfitters–many of which are stores that Broward shoppers would previously have to travel to Miami-Dade or Palm Beach Counties to enjoy. While you're here, bowl a strike at Bowlero, watch a movie at Regal, enjoy a glass of wine at Coopers Hawk, or dine at the other two dozen restaurants and eateries on the Dania Pointe campus. Just minutes from the airport, out-of-towners can also book a room at the AC Hotel Fort Lauderdale Airport or Marriott Fort Lauderdale Airport to enjoy their stay in Greater Fort Lauderdale with ease.

139 S Compass Way, Dania Beach, 833-800-4343
daniapointe.com

STEP INTO A CAMPER
TO SHOP PINK SLIP THREADS

Why have a brick-and-mortar store when you can just bring the goods with you? That's the philosophy behind Pink Slip Threads, where owner Karen Reinstatler peddles her groovy clothing, jewelry, and accessories from a 1974 vintage camper, affectionately known as The Deuce. While its origin story includes a storefront in Pompano Beach, the conversion to camper has turned the store on wheels into a welcome addition everywhere from art walks and fairs to bars and popups; Laser Wolf and Old Town Untapped in Pompano Beach are familiar haunts. When you're out and about, you'll probably see the store on wheels with its retro striping on the exterior, welcoming shoppers to explore oddities inside. To find out where Pink Slip Threads is going to be next, follow them on Instagram at @PinkSlipThreads_Mobile.

pinkslipthreads.com

DITCH ONLINE SHOPPING
FOR THE INDIE CRAFT BAZAAR

Remember being able to chat with the maker of a piece of jewelry before buying it? Shoppers in search of one-of-a-kind creations are in for a treat at the quarterly Indie Craft Bazaar in downtown Fort Lauderdale. More than 75 vendors take over the spaces at Revolution Live, Stache, and The Backyard for a mega market of handmade jewelry, vintage clothing, handmade body products, homemade treats, artwork, and accessories you never knew you needed. The free event also features food trucks, bars to provide libations while you shop, activities for patrons of all ages, fun contests, and pop-up experiences. The team who puts on the event also hosts a market during Hollywood Art Walk, Dania After Dark, and specialty holiday festivals—making handcrafted goods always within reach in Greater Fort Lauderdale.

100 Nugent Ave.
indiecraftbazaar.com

SEE A DRIVE-IN MOVIE
AT THE SWAP SHOP

Is it a flea market, carnival, car museum, farmers market, or drive-in movie theater? For the Swap Shop, the answer is "all of the above." Located on the stretch of Sunrise Boulevard that connects Fort Lauderdale with neighboring Lauderhill, Swap Shop provides a cacophony of activity behind the fence, with thousands of vendors bartering their wares, kids screaming with delight on carnival-style rides, and ticket sellers doling out spots for moviegoers. Owned by the Henn family, the Swap Shop got its start in 1964 as a one-screen drive-in. Now, the Swap Shop boasts 14 screens in the Thunderbird Drive-In Theater with tickets for just $7, a car museum (the late patriarch of the family loved to race), food and drink vendors, carnival rides, window tinters, and pretty much any item you can think of for sale.

3291 W Sunrise Blvd., Lauderhill, 954-791-7927
floridaswapshop.com

GET THE LOOK
AT ETIQUETTE BOUTIQUE

Shoppers in Fort Lauderdale know where the big-box clothing stores are, but fashionistas head to the small boutiques to get an original look. Etiquette Boutique is one of them, with a bevy of classic looks as well as more trendy, in-the-moment ensembles for a night out on the town or the beach. The owner, David Harris, found success in the clothing business in Nashville but yearned for South Florida living. He relocated to Fort Lauderdale and opened the first Etiquette location in 2012. Since then, he has expanded to three more locations in Broward and Palm Beach Counties with a fifth on the way in Dania Beach. If you fall in love with their clothing line, your shopping doesn't have to end when you head home from your trip to Fort Lauderdale—Etiquette has an online store, too.

2368 N Federal Hwy., 954-306-2837
1827 Cordova Rd., 954-652-1074
1400 Glades Rd., #150, Boca Raton, 561-717-8421
2596 PGA Blvd., Palm Beach Gardens, 561-249-2426

SUPPORT LOCAL ARTISTS
AT THE FLAMINGO FLEA

Every other month, Tarpon River Brewing is transformed into The Flamingo Flea, a market of vintage finds, upcycled goods, and handcrafted creations by local makers as well as live music, crafts, and dogs for adoption. Started in 2019, founder Carley Sumner has expanded to an impressive level with a northern Flamingo Flea at Crazy Uncle Mike's in Boca Raton (6450 North Federal Highway), monthly Meet the Makers events at Small Wine Shop (410 North Andrews Avenue in Fort Lauderdale), a Music & Makers Market at Friday Night Sound Waves, and pop-up events like Puppy Brunch and creator workshops. Between flea markets, check out the Flamingo Collective pop-up shop with a rotating list of artisans at Small Wine Shop. Whether you're shopping for yourself or purchasing a gift for a friend, you'll always be asked, "Where did you get that?"

280 SW 6th St.
flamingoflea.com

BUY BLOOMS
AT ANN'S FLORIST

A fixture on Las Olas Boulevard since the '70s, the family-owned Ann's Florist & Coffee Bar is a cozy cafe, flower shop, and boutique all in one. The space offers sidewalk and indoor seating to enjoy a cup of coffee, pastries, and dessert; or, during the afternoon and evening hours, order a glass of specially selected vino from the wine bar. Inside, the Victorian-inspired shop is filled with blooms from around the world as staff is hard at work creating breathtaking bouquets for special events or helping customers choose the right arrangements for that special someone. Walking through the floral shop, you'll also find unique gifts like greeting cards, stationery, candles, journals, needlepoint pillows, and tableware. Check their calendar for upcoming workshops, where you'll learn to make your own floral arrangements or flower crowns.

1001 E Las Olas Blvd., 954-761-3334
annsfloristlasolas.com

98

BRING THE OCEAN INTO YOUR HOME
WITH A GUY HARVEY PAINTING

Artist, conservationist, scientist, explorer—Guy Harvey can check a lot of boxes. His easily identifiable artwork is everywhere, from fishing shirts to the three-story mural at the Fort Lauderdale-Hollywood International Airport, and he has even painted an eponymous sunken ship off the coast of Fort Lauderdale that divers can explore. Collectors and fellow marine life enthusiasts can purchase his artwork at one of his few brick-and-mortar stores here on Fort Lauderdale's Las Olas Boulevard. Besides paintings of sailfish, sea turtles, and dolphins, items for sale include clothing and home goods. Since Harvey's company headquarters are also in Fort Lauderdale, you might even catch a glimpse of him stopping by from time to time.

816 E Las Olas Blvd., 844-842-7839
guyharvey.com/pages/las-olas-store

99

FIND WHIMSY
AT THE WANDER SHOP

Rattan furniture, clothing in earth tones, and walls covered in trees and pink and gold rainbows—The Wander Shop carries its own aesthetic. The store is known for its collection of fashions in cream, rust, yellows, white, dusty pink, and florals, but owner Marisa Folz has also stocked the shelves and bookcases with quirky wine labels, greeting cards, handbags, hats, and candles made by Florida creators. The Wander Shop made its way onto the fashion scene in Fort Lauderdale in the form of a 1963 Airstream Overlander, seen at The Yard in Wilton Manors and markets, but today it's a full-blown boutique in burgeoning Oakland Park. Its next-door neighbors include other small businesses, such as Rebel Wine Bar and The Butcher's Barrel, and it is just a few blocks away from Funky Buddha Brewery.

3548 NE 12th Ave., Oakland Park, 954-368-4647
thewandershop.com

100

SHOP FOR LADIES NIGHT
WITH SUNNY SIDE UP MARKET

Hidden on Fort Lauderdale Beach is Wine Garden, a secret getaway serving up wines and Italian fare—and playing host to the weekly Ladies Night market. Scheduled for every Wednesday evening, the women-run Sunny Side Up Market gathers local vendors for a sip and shop experience ($5 wines and $25 bottles!) at the outdoor restaurant as a part of its ongoing programming. But this is just one of the heavy schedule of events at Sunny Side Up, as their markets are also hosted at Pier 6, the Stranahan House, Society Las Olas, and the Mass District, to name a few, each one packed with shopping, live art and music, yoga, raffles, drinks, henna tattoos, pet adoptions, tarot card readings, and more.

sunnysideupmarket.com

Lorikeets at Butterfly World

ACTIVITIES BY SEASON

SPRING

SUMMER

FALL

WINTER

Jungle Queen has been a Fort Lauderdale fixture since 1935.

SUGGESTED
ITINERARIES

HISTORY BUFFS

LGBTQ GETAWAY

CONCERTS AND FESTIVALS

RIVERFRONT HAPPENINGS

OUTDOOR ENTHUSIASTS

One of the many colorful orchids
at the Bonnet House Museum & Gardens.

INDEX

• •

The Great Gravity Clock
at the Museum of Discovery and Science

Riding an air boat through the Florida Everglades.
Photo courtesy of Anthony J Rayburn, anthonyjrayburn.com